TROPICAL
AQUARIUM
FISH

TROPICAL
AQUARIUM
FISH

JOHN DAWES

NH
NEW
HOLLAND

Previous page:
**Platies and their close relatives, the swordtails, are
among the most popular of all tropical freshwater
aquarium species**

Opposite:
**Bloodfin Lyretail Swordtails, one of numerous
varieties of this species**

This edition first published in 2000 by
New Holland Publishers (UK) Ltd
London • Cape Town • Sydney • Auckland

24 Nutford Place, London W1H 6DQ, UK

80 McKenzie Street, Cape Town 8001, South Africa

14 Aquatic Drive, Frenchs Forest, NSW 2086, Australia

218 Lake Road, Northcote, Auckland, New Zealand

4 6 8 10 9 7 5 3

Distributed by Sterling Publishing Company, Inc
387 Park Avenue South, New York, NY 10016

Distributed in Canada by Sterling Publishing
c/o Canadian Manda Group, One Atlantic Avenue, Suite 105,
Toronto, Ontario, Canada M6K 3E7

ISBN 1 85368 579 8

Editor: Lydia Darbyshire
Designed and typeset by Jonathan Andrews Editions

Reproduction by Hirt & Carter, South Africa
Printed and bound by Times Offset (M) Sdn. Bhd.

CONTENTS

INTRODUCTION

The chances are that if you have never kept fish yourself, you will know of someone who has or does. Millions of people the world over share a passion for aquatic creatures and plants, and many of these take their interest further and actually attempt to keep, breed and propagate fish, invertebrates and plants in home aquariums.

One of the major challenges facing anyone who wants to enter this fascinating hobby is how to get started. There are numerous books on aquarium-keeping, dealing with all manner of subjects, from community aquariums to giant fish, the so-called "tank busters." But how do you actually decide what type of aquarium you need, or what branch of the hobby you should opt for? This book is intended to answer these questions.

It assumes no prior knowledge of the subject. Indeed, the only assumption it does make is that you have chosen a tropical, instead of coldwater, aquarium. It introduces the complete beginner to each major form of tropical aquarium-keeping by taking a brief look at aquatic life, highlighting the main characteristics, potential and limitations of each branch of the hobby. It then considers the criteria for choosing aquariums, how to set them up and maintain them in order to help the reader to make informed decisions regarding his or her choice at every stage.

By the end of the first two main sections, the new or prospective aquarist should be in a position to choose whether to select a freshwater, brackish or marine system. Any doubts that might linger can be settled by knowing what species of fish, invertebrates and plants suitable for beginners are likely to be available. These are therefore featured in the species guide in the last part of the book.

The first section of this guide covers recommended species for beginners. It is followed by a brief look at "second-level" species, which discusses fish and invertebrates that are widely available but that, ideally, should not be introduced into first aquariums. The third section, species for experienced aquarists, deals in general terms with those types that beginners would be wise to avoid. Finally, there are some suggestions for the most popular freshwater, brackish and marine plants available.

Aquarium-keeping is a tremendously exciting, rewarding and life-changing activity. It can also be hugely frustrating if the wrong decisions are made at the outset, and so it is with the aim of preventing newcomers to the hobby from making those wrong decisions that I have written this book. It is intended to help those who feel the urge to "dive" into aquatics to take those first tentative steps armed with a sound knowledge of exactly what they are embarking upon.

Welcome to the best hobby in the world!

John Dawes

**Lyretail Anthias with a school of Jacks
in the background, Indian Ocean**

PART 1

FISH IN NATURE

FISH IN NATURE

Fish have long fascinated mankind. Some fish achieve this effect through sheer size – the gentle whale shark, for example, can grow to an awe-inspiring length of over 39ft (12m.) Others are tiny. In fact, some are so minute that they are among the smallest vertebrates known to science. A leading contender for this "micro-title" is the minuscule and appropriately named pygmy goby, which, at full stretch, can span less than half an inch (10mm.)

Some species carry built-in lights, while others appear to have no eyes at all. Some are so brilliantly colored that they look garish to human eyes. Others are so unfishlike in appearance that they could easily be mistaken for fronds of sea-weed or algae-covered rocks. Yet others carry their own fishing-lines with them, luring unsuspecting prey to certain death. Some are power-houses of electricity; others will suck blood.

Many cast their eggs in millions and abandon them to the water, relying on chance alone for the survival of the species. A smaller number care intensely for their offspring, incubating the eggs in their mouths and even scooping up the babies (fry) and swimming away to safety at the first sign of danger. Another relatively small number retain the fertilized eggs within their bodies, later giving birth to fully formed young, which, as a result, have a much better chance of survival than the cast-off fry of the egg scatterers.

It seems that whatever permutation of color, shape, behavior and so forth we can possibly imagine, fish have already explored it through the forces of evolution. This relentless process means that today there are well over 20,000 species of fish that we know of, and, without doubt, many more remaining to be discovered. Equally certain is the fact that many species will remain undiscovered for all time.

HABITATS

With so many species in existence and so much of the world covered in water, it should come as no surprise to learn that fish have colonized virtually every aquatic niche that can be colonized. From the aquarium-keeping point of view, this is good news, of course, because this diversity offers us tremendously exciting and varied opportunities.

The majority of the thousands of species known are not what would be termed "aquarium fish," although several thousand can be kept and bred in aquariums. In this book, we will concentrate on some of the best-known and most widely available aquarium fish, under three main categories – freshwater, brackish water and marine. Before delving a little deeper into the biology of fish or their upkeep, however, a few explanations will not come amiss.

Freshwater or Marine

With relatively few exceptions, such as the salt lakes of Utah, the Dead Sea in Israel and the soda lakes of Africa, all bodies of water located within the major landmasses contain freshwater. Not all freshwater is the same wherever it is to be found, however. For example, the waters of the Amazon basin are termed soft and acid, while those of the African rift lakes are hard and alkaline. Soft and

A Jewel Cichlid displays the intense brood care characteristic of the cichlid family

acid waters contain relatively high concentrations of acidic compounds, such as those that are produced during the breakdown of vegetable matter. They also contain low levels of dissolved mineral salts. Hard, alkaline water, on the other hand, contains higher levels of dissolved salts and little, if any, of the acids that are generated in jungle-fed aquatic environments.

Despite their differences, all freshwater habitats have at least one thing in common: they contain no significant levels of sodium chloride, the main salt that makes marine habitats what they are. There are many other salts involved, of course, but sodium chloride is the most abundant and important.

Fish in nature are adapted to the specific water conditions they inhabit. They will require the water in an aquarium, therefore, to be as close as possible in composition to that of their natural habitat. In addition to what could be termed strict freshwater and marine environments, there is an in-between set of conditions, which exists as river courses approach the sea. Known as estu-

Redfin Butterfly

Mangrove terrain of the Red Sea coast

aries, these habitats are extremely fertile and are characterized by fluctuating levels of salinity, which become higher nearer to the sea or during high tide, and lower further inland or during low tide. Such freshwater/saltwater conditions are referred to as brackish. The fish, other animals and plants that inhabit this zone are characterized by exceptional powers of adaptation.

Although freshwater, brackish and marine conditions have been discussed separately, in reality they should be regarded as components of a continuous spectrum, one extreme of which is

African rift lake, Malawi

pure freshwater (i.e., of laboratory quality). Such pure water, which is used as the standard against which other types are measured, is said to have a specific gravity (SG) of 1.000. In nature, of

The differing types of water conditions shown as a continuous spectrum

Paradise Fish,
a "coldwater" tropical

and tropical is very difficult, if not impossible, to determine precisely. The goldfish, for example, is universally accepted as a coldwater fish. The guppy and the Cleaner Wrasse, on the other hand, are equally well known as tropical species, the former being a freshwater and the latter a marine one. The goldfish can, nevertheless, easily tolerate so-called tropical temperatures, while the guppy can survive in cool conditions that few would regard as being genuinely tropical.

If we were to adopt dictionary-type definitions, species that originate in countries that are situated between the Tropic of Cancer and the Tropic of Capricorn would be deemed tropical, while those originating outside this region would be excluded. This classification does work well most, but not all, of the time. For example, the Paradise Fish – the first so-called tropical species imported into Europe in 1869 – is found in parts of non-tropical China, yet it is widely regarded as a tropical fish and is, in fact, never sold as a coldwater species. Equally, other species, such as the White Cloud Mountain Minnow or the Mosquito Fish, are featured in most books on tropical fish.

A further potentially confusing factor is that, by definition, the tropics experience tropical temperatures throughout the year. In such countries, some of which excel at breeding fancy varieties of goldfish, there are, therefore, no such things as coldwater or tropical aquariums. All aquariums are, in essence, tropical, irrespective of what fish or other forms of life they may hold.

The term "native" is also quite often encountered within the hobby. There are, for example, "native marines" and "native freshwater species." Because these terms are generally applied to animals and plants that could be classified as "coldwater," they are, in reality, abbreviated ways of referring to species that are native to temperate countries. Species that are native to genuinely tropical countries cannot, of course, be coldwater in nature.

Despite the inherent problems with the use of the terms "coldwater" and "tropical," it would be wrong to assume that they have no real meaning or application. They must, however, be seen in context, forming elements of a continuous spectrum in much the same way as the terms "freshwater" and "marine" do.

As we move from the tropical end of this spectrum toward the center, the dividing lines become progressively blurred, until there is considerable doubt about the classification of those species whose temperature preferences are neither coldwater nor tropical. In some ways, such species could be regarded as "coldwater tropicals." The three fish mentioned above – Paradise Fish, White Cloud Mountain Minnow and Mosquito Fish – are perfect examples of species that tolerate coldwater, but there are

course, water is never pure. It always contains something or other dissolved in it, and the higher the concentration of solutes, the higher the SG. Soft, acid water, therefore, has a lower SG than hard alkaline water. Saltwater has an SG of approximately 1.020. This figure is pretty constant throughout the world, except where the sea in question is enclosed in some way or other – the Red Sea, for example – where the value is higher.

As we have seen, in between freshwater and marine environments lies brackish water, which is difficult to define in terms of SG. It is, in fact, quite impossible to allocate a fixed value to it, but we can say that any water whose specific gravity lies between 1.005 and 1.015 can be regarded as brackish. Values between 1.008 and 1.010 could be regarded as average; the lower the figure, the lower the concentration of saltwater and vice versa.

Coldwater or Tropical

Aquarium fish are classified in many different ways – for example, as freshwater/marine, livebearers/egglayers – or, in terms of temperature preferences, as coldwater/tropical.

At first sight, the distinction between temperatures appears quite straightforward and logical. However, as in the case of freshwater and marine conditions, the dividing line between coldwater others, details of which will be found in the species section.

A coldwater aquarium may be seen, in general terms, as one that does not require the provision of any form of heating, either for everyday maintenance, or for the breeding of its inhabitants. A tropical aquarium, by contrast, is one that requires additional heat for all-round, long-term success.

FISH BIOLOGY

Fish are highly complex creatures that have evolved over time into a myriad of forms, each beautifully in tune with its environment and each perfectly honed by the process of selection of the fittest to survive and breed, thus ensuring the continuation of the species from one generation to the next. The ways in which this is achieved are as diverse as the number of species in existence would lead one to believe. Yet despite the virtually endless variations on the basic theme, all fish share a number of characteristics. It is important to note, though, that in this book we are discussing bony fishes as opposed to cartilaginous fishes such as sharks, skates and rays. Very few of these are kept in aquariums, even by advanced hobbyists.

In trying to define a fish, we need to do away with the concept of a brief and infallible statement. Such a definition just does not exist. If we used the presence of scales to define a fish, other animals – reptiles, for instance – would fall within the definition. If we used the presence of gills, some amphibians would have to be included, and

Lemon Tetra showing the adipose fin, a small extra fin behind the dorsal fin which occurs in some species

so on. By far the best workable approach is to establish a list of characteristics that, taken together, will help us to identify an animal as a bony fish.

Thus, a bony fish is characterized by the possession of a braincase, a vertebral column (backbone) and a skeleton supporting the limbs. Respiration is by means of gills, although additional auxiliary structures may be used. These gills have external openings, consisting of slits in the vast majority of cases. Bony fish also have fins, although in some these are so highly modified as to be hardly recognizable. Most species are covered in scales; at least some of the scales extending down the midline of the body, from head to tail, carry sensory pits, collectively

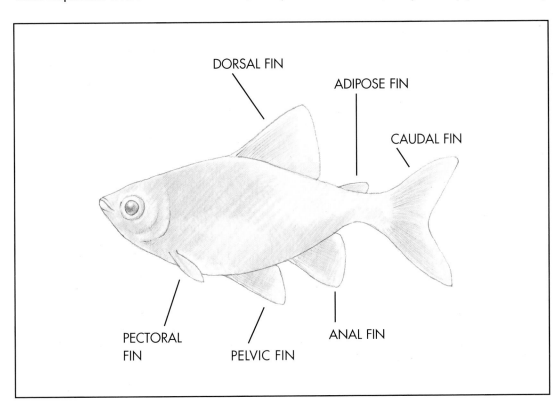

DORSAL FIN

ADIPOSE FIN

CAUDAL FIN

PECTORAL FIN

PELVIC FIN

ANAL FIN

The basic arrangement of fins. A fish usually has seven fins: dorsal, caudal, anal, two pelvic and two pectoral. Certain species also have an additional, "adipose" fin

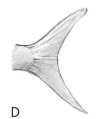

Tail fins:
A: Truncated
B: Crescent
C: Round
D: Lyre-shaped
E: Cleft

A   B   C   D   E

referred to as the lateral line organ. Buoyancy is controlled by a structure known as the swim or air bladder, but this may be absent in bottom-dwelling species. Finally, bony fish are, with only a few exceptions, poikilothermic. This term is often interpreted as meaning "coldblooded," but it actually means that the temperature of the blood matches that of the environment.

Like all animals, a fish needs to move, feed, breathe, reproduce, sense its environment, grow and generally do everything that is required to maintain life. To cover each of these subjects in detail would take up the total space available in this book, and a great deal more. From an aquarium point of view, however, some features have more direct visual impact than others, so a few words about them would seem appropriate.

Fins and their uses

Fins are marvelously flexible structures that are primarily concerned with movement and balance, but they can, and often do, have other functions.

The basic arrangement from which all subse-

quent modifications have developed consists of one dorsal (back) fin, one caudal (tail) fin, one anal (belly) fin, two pelvic (hip or ventral) fins and two pectoral (chest) fins. In addition, some fish, like the Characins (including the Piranha, Neon Tetra and numerous other well-known species), have a small adipose fin, sometimes referred to as a second dorsal fin, between the main dorsal fin and the tail.

Fish have evolved all manner of uses for this basic "equipment," ranging from straightforward locomotion and balance, to mating organs – such as the modified anal fin (the gonopodium) of male livebearers; wings – as in the enlarged pectorals of the flying fish; feelers – such as the thread-like pelvic fins of the Dwarf Gourami and its relatives; fishing rods, complete with lure – as in the anterior rays of the dorsal fin in anglerfish; venomous spines as found in the scorpionfish and stonefish; and countless other possibilities, many of which can be easily observed at close quarters in the home aquarium.

Mouths and Feeding

Just as there are predators and prey on land, so there are under water. Every conceivable method of obtaining food and every type of food itself seem to have been explored by fish.

There are predators as obvious and famous as piranha, barracudas and sharks, or as subtle and

A group of Congo Tetras. The mature male of this species has an elongated dorsal fin which will frequently overhang the caudal fin

Black Piranha showing the distinctive mouth of the predator. Both jaws contain sharp teeth, with the lower jaw projecting farther than the top jaw

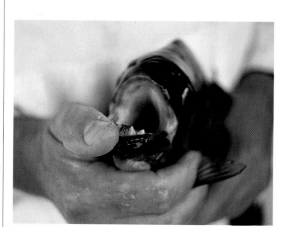

A   B   C

There are three main
types of mouth.
A: Superior, for surface-
feeders
B: Terminal for
midwater-feeders
C: Inferior for bottom-
feeders

surprising as the delicate Cardinal Tetras. Among the grazing fish are species such as the Sucking Loach (or Chinese Algae Eater) and the Suckermouth Catfish, which feed predominantly on algae, while among the more unusual fish are scale eaters, worm suckers, egg poachers and blood suckers.

Clues as to what food a species eats in the wild and where that food is found can often be deduced by studying the position, shape and size of the fish's mouth, the type, number and arrangement of teeth, and how the whole body is put together. A fish with an upturned mouth and a slim, torpedo-shaped body, for example, is likely to be a water-surface feeder, but one with its mouth on the underside of its head, a plate-like set of small, rasping teeth and a long, taper-ing body is likely to be a bottom scraper that lives in fast-flowing water.

With a little thought and study, it is a straight-forward matter to select a community of fish that will exhibit a range of feeding adaptations and behavior, thus adding an extra dimension to the home aquarium.

Breeding Strategies

Although fish can, in broad terms, be classified as either egglayers or livebearers, this simple distinction hides a whole range of differing repro-ductive strategies.

Dwarf Sucker Catfish feeding on algae

Egglayers, for instance, can scatter their eggs in open water, among vegetation or between rocks and gravel and leave nature to do the rest, or they can brood them in their mouths, thus offering them a considerable degree of protection. The eggs of the seahorse are actually carried by the male in a special abdominal pouch until they hatch – a rare case of paternal, rather than maternal, pregnancy. Some species lay their eggs in bubble-nests, others on stones, others on leaves. Others lay their eggs inside other organisms – the Bitterling lays eggs in the freshwater mussel, for example. A few even carry their eggs around embedded in their own skin.

Among the livebearers, there are those species that retain eggs within egg sacs inside the female's ovaries until they hatch. Others actually ovulate, almost like mammals, and even nourish their embryos during development.

In between egglayers and livebearers lies a fas-cinating range of fish that, like the livebearers, employs internal fertilization but then adopts the egglayers' technique of expelling the eggs from their bodies. They may then either carry them around for a while, like the Rice Fish or Medaka,

Jewel Cichlid laying its eggs

which can, but does not always, use internal fertilization, or deposit them immediately, like the Swordtail Characin.

Detailed information on how to breed fish has not been included in this book as it is outside the realm of the beginner. However, the species section at the end of the book includes notes on the breeding methods of each fish considered, as a general guide.

INVERTEBRATES

Invertebrates are animals that lack a backbone. Many of the more mobile types, like insects, or crabs, shrimps and lobsters, have jointed skeletons, but while this skeleton is internal among vertebrates, in invertebrates it is external. Many of the sedentary species, like the gastropods (snails) and bivalves (clams, cockles, mussels and so on) have shells rather than skeletons. Other sedentary types, like the hard corals, produce stony, calcareous outer skeletons, the characteristics of which are unique for each species. Still others, such as the related jellyfishes, do not produce a skeleton at all.

As in virtually every area of biology, there are "in-betweens" among the so-called invertebrates. These are creatures that, while being generally classed as invertebrates within the aquarium hobby, scientifically speaking lie somewhere between invertebrates and vertebrates: these are the Protochordates, sometimes referred to as the "first Chordates." The best known Protochordates are the fascinating, almost-unreal sea squirts or Tunicates, some species of which can be kept in aquariums. Sea squirts possess four important characteristics that separate them from the invertebrates and link them to the vertebrates. All four – a notochord (primitive spinal column), a dorsal, hollow, nerve tube, gill slits and a post-anal tail – are found in the tadpole-like larvae, but only the gill slits are retained by the adults.

It is estimated that something in the region of 97 percent of all living species of animals are invertebrates. Many of these are terrestrial and are, therefore, of little direct relevance to the home aquarium. This leaves, however, large num-

Sea squirts in the Indian Ocean

Louisiana Red Swamp Crayfish

bers of aquatic species, of which only relatively few are kept in aquariums, and only a fraction of those could be recommended for hobbyists.

On the whole, marine invertebrates are more demanding than fish, and they are certainly more demanding than their freshwater counterparts. Some, in fact, are so specific in their requirements – or we know so little about them – that even experienced aquarists have a difficult, sometimes impossible, job keeping them in peak health for any length of time. This presents us with a dilemma: if our present knowledge of such species is lacking in some way or if our current level of expertise is inadequate, we are not likely to be able to enjoy long-term success with them. If, however, we do not carry out any aquarium-based research into their upkeep, how are we going to progress? Among freshwater fishkeepers, for example, the Discus was once regarded as very difficult indeed. Yet today, provided the hard-learned lessons of the past are put to proper use and a few vital rules are followed, most aquarists can keep and breed Discus without any problems.

Although invertebrates as a whole are challenging, there are many species that are suitable for aquariums. Some of the shrimps, anemones, soft corals and sea squirts, for instance, can be kept successfully under conditions that are not difficult to establish and maintain, so there is no shortage of colorful, sensible choices, either for novices or more experienced aquarists.

Aquariums offer a never-ending stream of opportunities to enjoy, explore and learn about life under water. This has, of course, been true since fish were first kept in captivity. Today, however, the potential for the home aquarium is greater than it has ever been. Even once-difficult species of both fish and invertebrates can now be kept and bred without too much trouble thanks to the major advances made in knowledge and technology over the past 10 to 15 years.

PART 2

THE HOME AQUARIUM

THE HOME AQUARIUM

Previous page:
A "community" consisting of various species and varieties of barbs

COLLECTING AND FARMING

In the earliest days of aquarium keeping, most fish were collected from the wild. The most notable exceptions among coldwater fish were the many varieties of goldfish, while of the tropical species, guppies, mollies, swordtails and platies were among the first species to be regularly produced in commercial quantities. This situation soon changed as demand increased and the numbers of collectors soared, and even in the 1960s there was a reasonable crop of farm-bred species and varieties of freshwater fish available on the world market. Today, over 90 percent of all freshwater ornamental fish are bred specifically for the hobby and the percentage continues to increase as more and more captive-breeding programs are set up in countries as diverse as the U.S., Malawi, Singapore, the U.K., Sri Lanka and Israel, to name but a few.

As far as marine fish are concerned, the percentages are reversed, with over 90 percent of all "aquarium" species still being collected from the wild. Even this is changing, however, and a growing number of fish and invertebrates are now

A fish farm in Singapore

A fisherman collecting specimens from the Amazon

being bred in captivity. The best known of these are the various species of Clownfish, but farm-bred Damsels, Neon Gobies and even Marine Bettas (a type of grouper) now form part of the fast-expanding range of commercially produced species. In fact, about a hundred species of marine fish have already been bred, with varying degrees of success, in aquariums, and although translating this list into commercially viable programs undoubtedly presents major challenges, optimists firmly believe that we are beginning to get there. Driven by demands, both from consumers and the aquatic industry itself, improvements currently under way in aquarium technology, collecting, farming, handling, transportation and husbandry techniques, allied to the production of appropriate first foods for the tiny marine fish fry, should improve matters even further over the next few years.

LIMITATIONS AND RESPONSIBILITIES

Aquariums present us with ever-changing, colorful underwater pictures in our own homes, in the process teaching us about nature, the interdependence of living organisms, their needs and behavior, and even the fragility of life itself. Most aquariums, whether they are modest or massive in size, also offer exciting opportunities to make new scientific discoveries. Many formerly unknown aspects of the behavior of both fish and invertebrates have come to light through observations carried out by hobbyists and scientists in home and laboratory aquariums.

In addition, aquarium-based conservation programs to save threatened species of both freshwater and marine fish and invertebrate species can be, and are being, implemented all over the world. Particularly encouraging is the acceptance by scientists and academics that amateur aquarists can contribute significantly to such programs. As a result, a number of specialty aquatic societies now work with teams from museums, zoos and other institutions on the important task of trying to protect species as diverse as Mexican livebearers, African Haplochromine cichlids and seahorses from the many and varied threats currently facing them.

Having said this, however, it is important to stress that aquariums cannot provide us with solutions to all the challenges to which aquatic creatures are subjected. Their potential is enormous and constantly developing, but there are some limitations. No aquarium, however large

and well maintained it may be, for instance, can ever quite replicate conditions in the wild. Every time we enclose a body of water we are, by definition, isolating from the outside world that water and the animals and plants we place in it, and we thereby limit the number of interactions and processes that exist in nature. These would include the dilution of pollutants and waste products, the availability of supplies of new water, the natural relationships between predator and prey, naturally occurring food supplies and daily and seasonal fluctuations in day length, temperature, water flow and so on.

We also often house together unnatural communities of plants and animals. For example, Neon Tetras from the Amazon will be kept with Gouramis from India, or Rock Beauty Angelfish from the reefs of the western Atlantic with Black-footed Clownfish from the Indian Ocean. We might grow Ludwigia, a plant from the southern U.S., with Cryptocorynes from Malaysia. Such unnatural associations can, of course, be avoided relatively simply by selecting other animals and plants from prescribed regions. Even if we do this, though, we are most unlikely to choose a representative assemblage, either in numbers of individuals of each species or in the range of species that we can fit in the aquarium, or that are available to choose from in the first place.

Aquariums are, therefore, to varying degrees artificial creations, which are strictly under

Maroon Clownfish, a species originating in the Indian Ocean and ideal for a marine setup

human control. For all that, they are extremely valuable captive environments, and they can, with proper preparation and a good supply of common sense, provide conditions in which an extremely wide and expanding assortment of fish, plants and invertebrates can thrive and breed, protected from the threats that they would encounter in the wild.

In choosing to become aquarists, we take what is, potentially, a life-changing decision. We also take on the responsibility of controlling the lives of other living things. These creatures have no

Albino Tiger Oscar

choice in the matter, so it is our duty to provide them with the very best conditions that we can muster and that they, by right, deserve.

Fish may not wag their tails, bark or follow us around with unconditional loyalty as a dog does, but our responsibilities toward them are every bit as binding. Unless you are prepared to shoulder these responsibilities, therefore, you would be well advised to steer clear of aquarium keeping. Take on those responsibilities, however, and you are on the threshold of a new world, overflowing with experiences, the like of which few other activities can offer.

Having made the decision to become an aquarist, one of the first things you need to do is to discover what the various branches of the hobby entail and what aquarium choices are available so that you can decide which of these best fits your preferences and circumstances.

TYPES OF AQUARIUMS

Before we consider the actual shape and size of an aquarium – criteria that do play a part in the decision-making process and that will be dealt with later in this chapter – it is necessary to assess types of aquariums in terms of their water and inhabitants.

Basically, the choice is simple. Having settled on the fact that we are dealing with so-called tropical systems, the choice is among freshwater, brackish water and marine aquariums. For anyone thinking about becoming an aquarist, a visit to an aquatic shop can prove both fascinating and bewildering. With so many fish, plants and invertebrates to choose from, how does one make a start? And what do all the various bits of equipment do? And is the fact that shelves are full of water treatments, foods and remedies an indication that successful aquarium keeping demands a degree in biology, biochemistry or engineering, or all three? One thing is certain. Do not assume that your first visit to the aquatic shop will result in all your questions being answered and that you will acquire an aquarium and all its contents, including the fish and plants, in one go. Such a situation is now quite rare and thankfully it is getting rarer with each passing year. Nowadays, the emphasis is much more on discussing and resolving the important early questions before any purchases are made. The one thing to be avoided at all costs is the temptation to buy any livestock during the first visit. Good retailers will, in fact, not allow you to do this.

Despite the expert assistance that most shops can offer, it helps enormously if you have covered some of the early groundwork in advance and have, at least, considered some of the important initial decisions. Among the earliest steps is a consideration of which branch of aquarium keeping best fits your likes, needs and circumstances, so before you set foot inside an aquatic shop, think about the main characteristics of freshwater, brackish water and marine systems.

Freshwater Aquariums

The freshwater aquarium is the most popular system among tropical aquarium hobbyists. The reasons are many and varied, but perhaps the most important are, first, that freshwater tropical fish and plants are, generally speaking, the easiest of the three categories to keep; second, that many of the fish will breed easily in aquariums, and third, that there is no shortage of colorful, small, hardy and relatively inexpensive species and varieties to choose from.

Hardiness is a relative and somewhat misleading term because it depends on several factors. For example, some of the most popular tropical freshwater fish are the various mollies, yet some mollies tend to be regarded as a little delicate when they are compared with unequivocally "tough" types such as guppies. The reality is that mollies are pretty tough themselves, as long as they are provided with the conditions to which they are best suited. The wild species and a number of cultivated forms require water that is on the slightly hard, alkaline side, with a little salt added to it. In other words, mollies like slightly brackish conditions, yet they are generally regarded as freshwater tropicals.

Fortunately for first-time aquarium keepers, however, many of the modern captive-bred varieties have been cultivated for so many generations in freshwater that the above "rule" cannot be strictly applied to all mollies.

Within the overall umbrella term "tropical

Freshwater community aquarium

Discus are best suited to a species aquarium

chemistry, species selection and so on, needs to be a little more thorough.

For a list and brief details of some of the best known community fish, see Species for Beginners on page 47.

Brackish Aquariums

As we have already noted, brackish water contains varying amounts of salt. In nature, these conditions are found in estuaries, with or without accompanying mangrove swamp areas, and they are subjected to twice-daily fluctuations as the tides ebb and flow. The animals, too, vary at any given spot, since they tend to migrate up and down river according to their salinity preferences and tolerances. In the home aquarium such fluctuations are, at best, extremely awkward to replicate, so the degree of brackishness adopted is usually fixed at a level that makes life easier for both the aquarist and the plants and animals.

Broadly speaking, the brackish spectrum spans levels of specific gravity between about SG1.005 and 1.015 (see page 10). At the lower end, conditions are close to freshwater, while at the top end, they are not far from genuine marine conditions. This means the choice of species will have to be carefully thought out to take account of these differences. Although the range of both fish and plants available for stocking brackish aquariums is more limited than it is for freshwater or marine systems, the choice is still wide enough to

freshwater aquariums," two main categories can be identified. The first is the community aquarium, which, as the name suggests, consists of a number of species that can live in harmony with each other. The second is the species aquarium, which consists of a single species that, for reasons such as specific water requirements or behavior, cannot easily be kept with other species. The community aquarium is by far the more popular, especially among newcomers to the hobby, but again, the term "community" embraces a range of possibilities. For instance, the most frequently encountered communities are those in which a number of unrelated species with more or less flexible requirements and compatible behavior patterns are kept together. A suitable selection for such a setup could include guppies, Dwarf Gouramis, Bronze Corydoras, Catfish, Neon Tetras and/or Cardinal Tetras, a single male Siamese Fighter (two will fight, often to the death) and a couple of angelfish.

Other communities are designed for species that come from a specific type of environment, such as the African rift lakes. These species require hard, alkaline water and a tank layout with numerous calcareous rock caves. Even here, subdivisions could include fish species from the different lakes being kept together or aquariums that are dedicated to species from a particular lake, such as Lake Malawi or Lake Tanganyika.

Of all the available options, by far the easiest for a beginner is the "general" community aquarium. This is not to say that if your preference is for cichlids from the African rift lakes you must begin with something easier. It does mean, however, that your preparation with respect to water

The Mudskipper is one of the few species that require exclusively brackish conditions

permit an interesting collection. Most of the species kept will be those usually associated with freshwater aquariums with relatively fewer marine subjects, but a few species that are firmly identified as strict brackish species may be included and perhaps the most notable of these is the fascinating and unusual Mudskipper. A list of

Suggested layouts for (top) a marine brackish tank and (below) a "mangrove swamp" aquarium

recommended species is included in Species for Beginners on page 64.

At this stage, the important thing is to be able to decide on the two main types of brackish aquariums that are available. Mangrove swamp aquariums consist of a layout resembling mangrove habitats (although without the mud) and incorporate bogwood, rocks and some salt-tolerant plants and fish, most of which are more commonly associated with freshwater aquariums. "Marine" brackish aquariums consist of condi-

tions of higher salinity than the mangrove swamp system and include both plants and animals that can tolerate (or prefer) such an environment. Most of the plants and many of the fish that can be kept in mangrove-type aquariums cannot be kept in this type of aquarium.

Of the two possible types, mangrove swamp aquariums are considerably easier to maintain, particularly since the toxicity of some fish wastes, such as ammonia, is far higher under predominantly marine conditions than under freshwater ones. Closer monitoring is therefore essential in "marine" brackish setups.

Marine Aquariums

As we move beyond the top end of the brackish aquarium, we come into genuine marine conditions. The moment we do, a whole new world opens up, with stunningly colored fish and invertebrates that can take our breath away. The majority of these come from coral reef environments, and because whether or not we admit it, all of us are captivated by the images of a tropical underwater paradise, it is hardly surprising, and totally understandable, that so many new aquarists fall in love with the concept of owning a miniature coral reef in all its splendor.

However, before plunging in, as it were, several important questions need to be considered. For example, coral animals and plants come from one of the most stable habitats known to man, and they have evolved over time in tune with these unchanging conditions. As a result, the

Redfin Black Lyretail Sword. Its adaptability makes it an ideal beginner's fish

vast majority of species show remarkably little tolerance of deviations from the narrow band of environmental parameters that exist in and around coral reefs. In addition, ammonia, which is perhaps the number one killer of fish, is far more toxic in marine conditions than in freshwater. Even to the unpracticed eye, the distress exhibited by fish suffering from the effects of ammonia poisoning is immediately obvious. When it comes to invertebrates, though, a distressed clam looks very much like an undistressed one – until it is too late.

Generally speaking, marine organisms are more expensive than freshwater ones, and the replacement of, say, a single, not particularly expensive, butterflyfish can cost as much as, say, twenty Neon Tetras.

Bearing these and other factors in mind, many authors and established aquarists advise beginners to steer clear of marines until they have acquired some experience with their freshwater counterparts. Although such advice has much going for it, it does tend to create the impression that it is impossible for outright beginners to start off with marine aquariums.

This is not, in fact, the case. It is possible to opt for marines right from the start, but, in order to do so, the groundwork needs to be considerably more thorough than for freshwater systems.

There are three main types of marine aquariums:

● **fish-only aquariums**, consisting of a selection of fish species that can live harmoniously together
● **invertebrate aquariums**, consisting exclusively of a community of invertebrates and plants
● **mixed aquariums**, consisting of a well-chosen selection of fish, plants and invertebrates.

Of these three types, the easiest ones to maintain are fish-only aquariums, because although marine fish are less tolerant of unfavorable environmental conditions than their freshwater cousins, they are more tolerant than marine invertebrates. Special diets, lighting requirements and compatibility are just three of the many factors that need to be taken into account in every type of aquarium, but particularly in those in which invertebrates are housed. It is, therefore, sensible (although not absolutely

A mixed marine aquarium

necessary) to begin with fish-only systems, moving on to invertebrates once some experience has been gained.

Of the three types, mixed systems (often also referred to as "reef aquariums") are by far the most difficult, because the requirements of both fish and invertebrates need to be provided for in a single tank. One of the major difficulties that beginners tend to experience with mixed systems is that many of the medications available for treating fish that fall ill are lethal to invertebrates. Compatibility among inhabitants is another major factor where such systems are concerned. It would, therefore, make sense to view mixed/reef aquariums as something to aim for, once an apprenticeship has been served in the keeping of both the other branches of marine aquariums.

SELECTING AN AQUARIUM

In the opening section of Part 2, the potential and limitations of aquariums were briefly mentioned. One of the features that limit their potential is the fact that, no matter how large or small a particular tank may be, it will contain water that, by definition, will be cut off from the outside world except where the water meets the air. The size of the available surface area for the exchange of gases is, therefore, of great importance.

Other criteria to consider when selecting tanks are their shape, what they are made of, how they are made and their overall appearance.

Size

An impressive freshwater tropical aquarium

One of the characteristics of enclosed bodies of water is that the smaller they are, the more susceptible they are to fluctuations in quality.

A freshwater community aquarium

Take, for example, a bucket and a cup, both filled at the same instant with boiling water. It is obvious that the water in the cup, because of the much reduced volume, will cool down a lot faster than the water in the bucket. Exactly the same applies to aquariums, except that in this case, a host of environmental parameters, not just temperature, are of importance.

Fish and invertebrates, for example, generate waste products, but these cannot be "flushed" away in a tank as would normally happen in a river or on a reef, so, in effect, all the inhabitants of the tank will end up breathing and swimming around in their own toxic excreta. This sounds worse than it is, provided that the wastes can be effectively taken care of. An adequate filtration/purification system will do this, but because the

AQUARIUM WATER CAPACITY						
Aquarium size	Approximate furnished volume				Weight of water	
	cu ft	liters	U.S. gals	U.K. gals	lb	kg
18x10x10in/45x25x25cm	0.95	27.3	7.2	6	60	27.3
24x12x12in/60x30x30cm	1.92	54.6	14.4	12	120	54.6
36x12x15in/90x30x38cm	3.20	91.0	24.0	20	200	91.0
48x12x15in/120x30x38cm	4.80	136.5	36.0	30	300	136.5
60x18x18in/150x45x45cm	11.20	318.5	84.0	70	700	318.5
72x18x18in/180x45x45cm	12.80	364.0	96.0	80	800	364.0

larger the volume of water available, the greater the inherent "cushioning" qualities against harmful fluctuations, it follows that large aquariums are able to handle wastes and other toxins more effectively than small ones.

When choosing an aquarium, therefore, it is always wise to go for the largest possible model that can be afforded or fitted into the available space. In general, the smallest freshwater tropical aquarium should measure around 24 x 24 x 12in (60 x 30 x 30cm). For marines, the smallest recommended size of tank for beginners is 36 x 15 x 12in (90 x 38 x 30cm).

Aquariums can usually be built to any specification, within reason, so if the available space measures somewhere between the above but is rather awkward, it will almost certainly be possible to have a customized aquarium built to fit. However, such aquariums tend to be more expensive than ready-made, commercially produced models. The table above lists some of the standard sizes of aquariums currently available, with an indication of their approximate capacities and the weight of water they contain.

Shape

Aquariums are available in all sorts of shapes, ranging from traditional rectangular ones to tall, multisided designs resembling columns of water. Choosing between them is not easy, particularly if you are about to buy your first aquarium, but keeping the following points in mind will undoubtedly help.

At the beginning of this section, reference was made to the air/water interface and to the importance of surface area with regard to gaseous exchange. This is the most important single factor that should be borne in mind when choosing the shape of an aquarium.

Fish, plants and the majority of other living organisms depend on oxygen (O_2) for their survival. Equally, most organisms find carbon dioxide (CO_2), one of the by-products of respiration, toxic. During daylight hours or in the presence of artificial light, green plants use carbon dioxide in a complex process known as

photosynthesis to produce food and generate oxygen. Some of this oxygen is used by the plants themselves in respiration, but the surplus is released into the surrounding water. The micro-algae that exist within the tissues of many invertebrates also do this. However, fish, along with the invertebrates themselves that "house" symbiotic green algae, are incapable of utilizing carbon dioxide.

Oxygen levels can quickly become dangerously low and carbon dioxide dangerously high (particularly at night) unless remedial or preventive steps are taken. As dissolved oxygen is used up, fresh supplies need to be made available, and as carbon dioxide is generated, the excess needs to be eliminated.

This is where surface area comes in. Clearly, the larger the surface area, the more efficient the exchange of gases will be. Turbulence, produced by means of air pumps or currents from powerhead or filter outlets, will help the process along,

A tank of Mosquito fish (*Gambusia affinis*), the most widely distributed livebearer in the world

Adult French Angel, large and demanding but truly impressive

but having an adequate surface area in the first place is critical.

With this in mind, it follows that if two differently shaped aquariums contain the same volume of water, and other parameters are equal, the one with the larger surface area will be more efficient at maintaining a satisfactory equilibrium of gases.

Glass or Acrylic

Glass is the traditional material used for constructing aquariums. Its transparency, flawless surface, durability and relative strength have combined to establish it as the top choice throughout the history of aquarium-keeping. Its major drawback is its inflexibility, which dictates that all sides of an aquarium must be straight. Although this does not restrict us to four-sided

An excellent use of bogwood in the home aquarium

aquariums, it does mean that every sheet must be attached to its neighbors, producing "seams" that some people find intrusive.

For many years, there were no alternatives to glass. Perspex, which was inexpensive, was usually used only for small aquariums such as those used in laboratories. Perspex also yellowed quickly and scratched easily. Nowadays, modern acrylic aquariums do not suffer from these problems to any significant extent, and acrylic tanks tend to stand up to inadvertent knocks better than all-glass models. Nevertheless, acrylic is still more easily scratched than glass, although scratch-removing kits are available. Multisided units, constructed out of a single piece of acrylic, are also considerably more likely to suffer from distortion than all-glass aquariums. Despite this apparent disadvantage, acrylic is more "flexible" than glass and can, therefore, be molded into shapes that are impossible with glass.

Overall Appearance

Aquariums, whether all-glass or acrylic, are sold either on their own – i.e., as tanks – or as part of a furniture unit – i.e., as cabinet systems.

Free-standing or "loose" tanks can be bought with a variety of trimmings that hide the bare glass edges – the old-type angle iron aquariums are hardly ever seen today – but these trimmings do not usually provide a great deal of support for the panes of glass. This is, however, unnecessary because of the exceptional bonding strength of modern silicone aquarium sealants.

Individual tanks have the undoubted advantage of being considerably cheaper than cabinet units. Hoods and other forms of cover can be bought independently or as an integral part of the unit. Another advantage of these tanks is that the aquarist has time to develop the system over a period of time, adding or replacing equipment as circumstances and experience allow.

Cabinet aquariums, on the other hand, come either in a "basic" form consisting of a cabinet, an aquarium and matching hood, or as a complete system, which includes all the necessary equipment as well. One great advantage of a complete system over the individual tank arrangement is that such cabinets come almost ready to plug in (note the use of the word "almost"). Another is that all the equipment is hidden from view.

Cabinets are also built with the considerable weight that they need to support taken into account. Water weighs about 8.3lb per gallon (1kg per liter). Add the weight of the tank itself, plus gravel and rocks, and it soon becomes apparent that a furnished aquarium, even of modest dimensions, is a very heavy item indeed. If you choose to buy a tank on its own, therefore, you must bear this in mind and make the necessary provisions, either by purchasing a

APPROXIMATE HEATER WATTAGE REQUIRED		
Size of aquarium in	cm	Power wattage
18x10x10	45x25x25	30 – 60
24x12x12	60x30x30	75 – 100
36x12x15	90x30x38	100 – 150
48x15x15	120x38x38	120 – 180
60x18x18	150x45x45	150 – 210

proper aquarium stand or by ensuring that the furniture on which the aquarium is going to sit is strong enough to support it.

Before deciding which option to select, visit a well-stocked aquatic shop and talk with a number of the sales staff. This will be well worth the effort, because a mistake at this early stage can prove disastrous.

EQUIPMENT

It seems that not a single month goes by without some new form of aquarium hardware becoming available. Essentially, however, as long as the basic requirements of the organisms we are planning to keep can be provided, refinements can come at a later stage. The minimum requirements are that tropical plants and animals require water that is of an appropriate temperature and chemical composition, is adequately illuminated and contains a good supply of oxygen.

Heating

As far as heating is concerned, the priority must be to choose a unit that is capable of comfortably maintaining the desired temperature but that has capacity to spare.

Whether you opt for separate heater and thermostat units, a combined system, heating plates, undergravel heating cables or a filtration unit with a built-in heating element will depend on your preferences and funds. The most popular units are the combined heater/thermostats because they are durable, easy to install and to adjust and are modestly priced. Before you decide, though, visit a good shop and look at the range available. Read the packaging, which usually gives an indication of what size of aquarium the unit has been designed for and speak to a member of the staff.

Lighting

This is a subject on which a knowledgeable member of the staff is worth his or her weight in gold to an aquatic shop.

When it comes to freshwater aquariums, the question of lighting is a little less involved than with marine invertebrates. Nevertheless some general guidelines apply to both. If you plan to keep an aquarium primarily to house fish and will not be attempting to grow plants or keep marine invertebrates, the final choice will largely depend on the fluorescent color (wavelength) you prefer, and on how much of it you want to provide.

If, however, you will be attempting to grow plants, either in a freshwater or marine setup, their needs will have to be taken into consideration. It is vital to provide the correct level of lighting for plants, in order for them to photosynthesize. There are numerous types of bulbs and fluorescent tubes currently on the market, so you should not encounter too many difficulties in finding something suitable, If there is a difficulty, it is in choosing from the extensive range that you are likely to come across, which is where a

APPROXIMATE LIGHTING REQUIREMENTS

Length of aquarium in cm		Freshwater fish only	Planted aquariums	Marine fish only	Invertebrate aquariums *
		Fluorescent lights	Fluorescent tubes 3,300 – 5,300K	Fluorescent tubes 5,500 – 6,500K	
18	4	1 x 8W	2 x 8W	–	–
24	1	1–2 x 18W	2–3 x 18W	–	–
36	90	1–2 x 20–30W	2–3 x 20–30W	1–2 x 30W	5 x 30W or 2 x 70W metal halide lamps
48	120	1–2 x 30W	3–4 x 30W or 2 x 80–125W mercury vapor lamps	1–3 x 30W	4–7 x 30W or 1 x 150W metal halide lamp
60	150	1–2 x 40–65W	3–4 x 40–65W or 2 x 125W mercury vapor lamps	2–3 x 40–65W	5–8 x 40–65W or 2–3 x 150W metal halide lamps

* For invertebrate aquariums the use of additional actinic lighting is recommended
It must be stressed that these figures are only broad guidelines. The dimensions and inhabitants of the aquarium may dictate otherwise, or other suitable arrangements may be proposed on the advice of a suitably qualified member of the staff or aquarist experienced in the keeping of specific types of fish, invertebrates or plants.

knowledgeable member of the sales staff can be so valuable.

The most critical choice of all is the one that must be made if you want to keep marine invertebrates. Many species, such as corals, certain types of mollusks and some anemones, are either entirely or partially dependent for their survival on unicellular algae, called zooxanthellae, which they contain within their tissues. Unless the level and quality of lighting takes account of this, the algae will die and so will the invertebrates. Of particular use to the well-being of invertebrates are actinic blue fluorescent tubes, which emit both blue and ultraviolet light, but these must be provided in addition to, and not instead of, other lighting.

Aeration and Filtration

Although aeration can be achieved completely independently of filtration, the topics have been combined here because many filters provide built-in facilities for oxygenating aquarium water. The critical factor in aeration is surface water turbulence, which will facilitate the uptake of oxygen (O_2) and the elimination of carbon dioxide (CO_2). To some extent, the way in which this is achieved is irrelevant, as long as it does not cause injury or stress to the aquarium inhabitants.

Aquarium aerators – more commonly referred to as air pumps – generally do their job by producing a stream of air, which is channeled centrifugally or by means of a diaphragm or by a piston drive, through an air line joined to one or more diffuser stones or small wooden blocks, which break up the stream into bubbles as it is forced through the pores of the diffusing materials. These bubbles create more of an illusion of aeration than actual aeration, although the smaller the bubbles – those produced by marine aquarium diffuser stones, for instance – the higher their aeration qualities as they rise to the surface. The main benefit derived from bubbles, however, derives from the surface turbulence they create.

Air pumps are generally rated either by the volume of air they produce per minute, or by the number of diffuser stones they can operate simultaneously in a given depth of water. Again, as for other items of aquarium hardware, seek professional advice when you are choosing from the wide selection available.

Filters can also serve as aerators, either because the stream of bubbles that drives the air-operated models rises through an uplift tube, thus disturbing the water surface, or because the stream of water produced by electrically operated models splashes on the water surface – for example, by means of a spray bar. A growing number of electrically operated filters (known as power filters) also have a built-in device called a

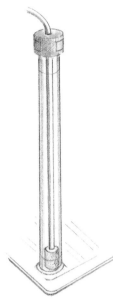

Air is released at the base of the airlift tube in an undergravel filter

"venturi," which sucks in air and mixes it with the water stream as it is driven through on its way back to the aquarium, thereby assisting with aeration. "Venturis" are also common features on powerheads, which are electrically operated water pumps usually fitted to the top of the air-lifts of undergravel filters.

Filters come in all shapes, sizes and, of course, prices, but all are designed to sieve out solid wastes from aquarium water. Most will also perform other functions, such as the biological purification (detoxification), by means of beneficial bacteria, of water laden with soluble wastes such as the ammonia produced by fish and invertebrates. Chemical purification is also possible if the filter is of the canister type. This takes place through adsorption by means of a suitable medium such as activated charcoal or zeolite (a clay-based material) held in the way of the flow of water passing through the filter.

Despite the undoubted sophistication of certain models, filters can be classified into the following categories:

● **Undergravel filters**, in which a plate, or set of plates, or a series of perforated tubes is laid under the gravel of the aquarium. These filters can be operated using an aerator, a powerhead or the flow from a canister-type power filter.

● **Box filters**, in which the water is driven through a box that can be situated either within the aquarium itself, or suspended on the outside. Internal models are air-operated, while external ones can be operated by either air or electricity.

● **Sponge/foam filters**, in which the water is sucked through a layer of sponge or foam by an air stream from the aerator.

● **Canister power filters**, in which water is electrically driven through a container holding one or more filter mediums. There are both internal and external models.

● **Trickle or wet/dry filters**, in which water is trickled through an external medium exposed to the air during at least part of the journey from and to the aquarium.

The main aim of a filter is to maintain water in good condition. It is this quality that determines whether or not a particular fish, invertebrate or plant will survive. Water quality is so important that it is safe to say that if we look after the water, the water will look after our aquarium plants and animals. It is therefore essential to have a clear understanding of the process of filtration/purification/detoxification – preferably before you actually buy a filter.

A detailed discussion of filtration is outside the scope of this book, but it is essential to consider briefly the types of filtration (as opposed to type of filter) and a few of the main types of filter medium.

● **Mechanical filtration** removes solid particles of waste and debris from the water. Whatever medium is chosen for the purpose, it acts as a sieve. Filter floss, sponge, foam, brushes and many other mediums are suitable choices, and in the case of undergravel filters, the gravel itself can act as this sieve.

● **Chemical filtration** removes toxic chemicals such as ammonia via adsorption (not absorption) onto a porous surface. The best known compounds for this are activated charcoal and zeolite, although there are others.
   Warning: zeolite removes ammonia and can be "recharged" by being soaked in salt solution. When this is done, the ammonia is released into the water. Because of this property, zeolite cannot be used in marine aquariums, because in these conditions, it is quite incapable of removing toxic ammonia.

● **Biological filtration** removes dissolved wastes through the action of beneficial bacteria. The process of detoxification begins with *Nitrosomonas* bacteria taking in ammonia and converting it to nitrites, which are also toxic to fish and invertebrates. Fortunately, *Nitrobacter* bacteria then convert these nitrites into relatively harmless nitrates. This process is known as nitrification.

It is also possible, with a little planning and by choosing the right medium, to keep nitrates under control by means of other types of bacteria, which will convert them back to free, harmless nitrogen that then disperses into the air at the water surface. This process is known as denitrification.

Just as there are different types of filtration or detoxification, there are different types of mediums. One thing that needs to be borne in mind, however, is that clear-cut divisions do not really exist, in the sense that if a medium is designed, say, to act primarily as a mechanical one, it will – to a greater or lesser extent – still develop a biological capability over a period of time as its surface becomes colonized by bacteria. The extent to which surfaces can be colonized determines how effective a medium will be in terms of biological efficiency. When choosing such a medium, therefore, it is important to consider the percentage of available surface that it contains for potential colonization, rather than its total surface area. Gravel, for example, has few, if any, pores and the available surface area is virtually the same as its total surface area. In sintered glass mediums, however, "porosity" is one of the most important features, and it therefore follows that sintered glass is a much more efficient biological medium than gravel.

The advantages of sintered glass and of some other biological mediums go even further, because the pores that lie deep within each cylinder, granule or block of medium are exposed to lower levels of oxygen than the outer ones and can therefore denitrify as well as nitrify at the same time. As a result such mediums are not only efficient at keeping levels of ammonia and nitrites down but also help in keeping nitrates under control.

Water Monitoring Equipment

These items are often regarded as accessories, but if the water quality is inadequate, successful aquarium-keeping is out of the question. It would, therefore, seem sensible to regard the following items as "essential" rather than as "desirable."

● **Thermometers** are available in all sorts of designs, from spirit-filled floating models, to liquid crystal, externally mounted strips or extremely accurate electronic maximum/minimum types. Take your pick, but do get one right at the outset.

The heater-thermostat automatically switches off the heat when the desired temperature is reached, and switches on again when it falls below the required level

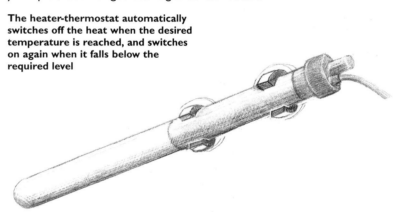

● **Test kits** have risen from the ranks of the "desirables" to that of the "essentials," and fish, plants and invertebrates the world over have benefited as a result. There are numerous types available for assessing everything from dissolved oxygen levels to the iron content in water. The minimum all aquarists should aim for are the test kits for: pH (alkalinity/acidity), ammonia, nitrites and nitrates. In addition, marine aquarists should also buy a copper test kit (copper is lethal to invertebrates, and testing for its presence is, therefore, of prime importance in such aquariums).

● **Hydrometers** are essential for all marine aquarists and highly desirable for those contemplating brackish water aquariums. Hydrometers measure salinity in terms of specific gravity.

Aquarium Accessories

Trying to determine which of the other items required to run an aquarium efficiently are essential pieces of equipment – and which are merely desirable – could lead to an unnecessary debate that, while interesting, would not help to make matters more manageable. Therefore, for the sake of convenience, they are included here under the umbrella title of Aquarium Accessories. Even though this list, which is not in any order of priority, cannot be considered all-encompassing, it will, at least, identify the main areas that are worth consideration.

Carpet anemones make ideal territory for Clownfish

AQUARIUM ACCESSORIES

ITEM	SOME USES
Spare bag of marine salt	Particularly useful for unexpected partial water changes (not for topping off purposes)
Protein skimmer	Hardly ever used (at present) in freshwater aquariums; extremely useful in marine aquariums for helping to control water-polluting organic compounds
Ozonizer	Used in conjunction with a protein skimmer, it improves the effectiveness of the water purification process and will also help control some disease-causing (pathogenic) organisms
Ultraviolet sterilizer	Will help to kill small, disease-causing organisms, including bacteria, and will also destroy algal spores and therefore help to control algal blooms
Spare inexpensive aerator	Temporary replacement in case of breakdown, particularly in aquariums with under gravel filtration
Nonreturn air line valve	Will prevent water siphoning back into aerator when/if this is switched off
T and Y pieces	Make a variety of air line arrangements possible
Air line	As an addition to, or replacement for, existing arrangement or new aquariums
Air line clips	Method of controlling rate of air flow through air lines
Spare diffusers	Those in use can become clogged under certain water conditions, lose efficiency or deteriorate at the joint between air line and diffuser
Spare diaphragm	Diaphragm in use may tear without warning; prompt replacement is essential
Range of fuses	In the case of electrical malfunction, fuses in plugs may blow; the range kept in reserve should match that of the plug in use
Cable tidy	Method of keeping wiring neat and safe
Gravel pad	Method of keeping layers of gravel separate from each other (very useful in marine aquariums) or from undergravel filter plates
Insulating/waterproof tape	Means of protecting electrical connections and aquarists
Heater-stat clips	Those in use can sometimes deteriorate or break during routine maintenance
Spare heater-stat fully wired up	This is essential – it may never be required but if/when it is, its value becomes self-evident
Range of nets	Should include small fine nets for transferring or catching fry and young fish, large fine ones for delicate species and coarser ones in a variety of sizes for more robust species

ROCKS, GRAVEL AND DECORATIONS

Submerged plants, which are also referred to as oxygenating plants or, simply, oxygenators, can absorb at least part of their nutrient requirements through their leaves. Many of the fine-leaved aquarium species can absorb most of their nutrients in this way. This ability has probably been one of the key factors contributing to the general lack of attention given to the nature of aquarium substrata in the past. Yet the bottom material, rocks and decorations are all vitally important components of an aquarium, and they can often determine how successful or otherwise an aquarium will be. Time spent considering the main options, therefore, will pay rich dividends in the end.

Gravel and Rooting Mediums

Gravel has tremendous advantages in that it is widely available, is easily washed before use, does not tend to pack into a solid, anaerobic – i.e., oxygen-deficient – block, can be bought in a range of grain sizes and is cheap. As a general type of substratum for freshwater community aquariums, gravel is by far the most popular of all the bottom mediums. As long as it is lime-free, it can be used in the vast majority of freshwater systems that do

AQUARIUM ACCESSORIES

ITEM	SOME USES
Breeding trap	Method of confining/protecting a pregnant livebearing female and her fry during birth and until appropriate accommodation for the young can be made available; all models provide a means of keeping the female, which will often eat her offspring, and the fry apart
Jam jars	Useful for transferring adult fish and fry, for very temporary quarters for fry, for treatment chambers and for a multitude of other useful functions
Pair of long forceps	Useful for removing dead fish and plants and objects from an aquarium; can double as planting stick
Planting sticks	Self-explanatory
Waterproof marker pen	Writing details of species, treatments administered, spawning, etc., on tanks
Algae cleaner/scraper	Means of keeping sides of tanks free of encrusting algae; magnetic cleaners allow the job to be done without getting one's hands wet
Siphon tube	Used for changing water; the tube should be at least as long as the distance between the rim of the tank and the floor, plus the height/depth of the tank
Gravel cleaner/dip tube	Useful for cleaning localized accumulations of debris or uneaten food that do not require a partial/major water change
Screwdrivers	Standard and star-tipped types should be kept handy for wiring plugs and maintaining/cleaning/stripping down electrical equipment. (Make sure that you are familiar with the correct methods of dealing with electricity and take all plugs from the sockets before you begin work)
Scissors	Useful for cutting airlines, insulating/waterproof tape and the like
pH adjusters	Useful methods of altering the acid/base balance of the water to suit particular species
Remedies for common diseases	Should be regarded as an essential safeguard but not resorted to as a matter of habit – prevention is better than cure
Small reserve stock of food	Useful means of overcoming oversights
Worm feeding ring	Restricts Tubifex worms to a relatively small area and minimizes the risks of widespread distribution of uneaten worms
Tube of silicone-based sealant	Emergency repair of leaks; also for attaching bark/bogwood to plastic/glass plates, which can then be covered with gravel to prevent them from floating

not require hard, alkaline conditions.

Gravel does have some drawbacks, however. It is, for instance, a totally sterile medium which, as a result, contributes no nutrients whatsoever to those plants that need to obtain nourishment through their roots. In time, particles of organic debris and so forth will become trapped between the gravel grains and thus provide some food sources for such plants, but at least until that point is reached, supplementary feeding with aquarium fertilizers of one kind or another is advisable. Other methods of improving the "nutritional" qualities of gravel include the use of subgravel peat/loam bags and plant "plugs," but these are not suitable for aquariums housing species that either dig or burrow.

Gravel that contains calcareous material is suitable for marine aquariums as well as aquariums housing species of fish and plants that prefer alkaline conditions, such as species of cichlid from the rift lakes of Africa. The most calcareous of all gravels/sands are the so-called coral sands, which are ideal for marine aquariums and high-saline brackish systems. Many aquarists who keep rift lake cichlids have also traditionally used such sand for their hard, alkaline aquariums, but the practice is now frowned upon by a growing number of aquarists. The argument is that the continual rooting about of sand-sifting species constantly raises clouds of the fine sand, which are probably one of the main causes of gill irritation in those species that are not equipped to handle these suspended particles. The modern trend is to use only a small percentage, 10 to 20 percent, of coral sand in most aquariums housing African rift lake species, except in those aquariums exclusively reserved for sand-sifting species, which require a fine substratum consisting of sand-sized, rather than gravel-sized, grains.

Another substratum widely available for marine aquariums is coral "gravel" or "chips" – small,

rounded fragments of dead corals found on all coral beaches and coral lagoons. This medium is particularly useful as the first layer above undergravel plates in marine systems, separated from a finer top layer of sand by a gravel pad.

Whatever type of gravel or sand you are buying, avoid sharp, angled mediums with ragged edges. These pose a real threat of injury to fish and invertebrates, particularly those that sift or burrow through the substratum in search of food or in the process of constructing a nest. In addition, find out if the gravel or sand contains calcareous material. You can do this by adding a drop of acid. If there is any calcium carbonate in the medium, it will fizz. Most people do not have any ready access to acid, of course, and you can, instead, add a little vinegar, which contains acetic acid. The reaction will be a little slower, but it will be strong enough to allow an accurate assessment to be made.

Rocks and Bogwood

Even in aquariums where the fish and/or invertebrates are open-water swimmers, rockwork or submerged pieces of bogwood will add considerably to the beauty of the aquascape.

Inert rocks, like slate, will have no effect on water conditions and are therefore safe to use in all systems. Bogwood, on the other hand, releases tannins, and it is, consequently, better suited for aquariums housing species that prefer soft acid conditions, such as most Amazon fish. This does not mean that bogwood cannot be used in other aquariums, but it does mean that the pieces will need to be sealed with, for example, several coats of polyurethane varnish to prevent them from releasing tannic acid into the water (remember to allow the varnish to dry between coats). Sealing will also prevent the tannins from coloring the water. The golden-amber colored staining that is produced by bogwood is, however, perfectly safe for a whole host of species – indeed, the waters of the Rio Negro in the Amazon basin are all tannin-stained.

The specific water requirements of some freshwater and marine community or species aquariums demand the use of particular types of rock. Tufa rock, which is softish, calcareous and light, is, for instance, especially suitable for aquariums housing species that prefer hard, alkaline water or for marines. Limestone is another appropriate choice for such systems.

Choosing one type of rock in preference to another does not, of course, mean that one cannot combine different types. In fact, in some aquariums, a mixture of rocks, some providing caves, and others providing smooth, horizontal or vertical spawning surfaces in the open, are a distinct advantage and increase the range of species that can be kept.

In marine aquariums, there is yet another

Living rock is a suitable choice for marine aquariums, especially for those already established

Broken pots and other decoration provide good homes for a variety of species

Decorations

Because a decoration, strictly speaking, is an item that adorns in one way or another, there is no need for it to perform any role other than an aesthetic one. Such a view of aquarium decorations does not, however, do justice to the range of products currently available to hobbyists.

There is a whole range of treasure chests, skulls, skeletons, galleons and all manner of ceramic products designed specifically to add a little touch of the unusual to an aquarium. Purists often criticize such decorations as "trivial" and "gimmicky," but there is absolutely nothing wrong with these items if they add to your personal enjoyment and, if the products are made out of safe, nontoxic materials (which they are), the fish will not mind one bit.

One step from the purely aesthetic decorations are those that have built-in uses, such as an outlet for an air line. Many of these functional decorations are hinged so that they open and close as the bubbles build up inside and are subsequently released.

The development of safe resins some years ago gave the aquarium decoration industry something of a boom, which resulted in a veritable explosion of items, from simulated logs to rocks and corals. While, at first, some of these products were less than convincing, the latest ones, especially at the more expensive end of the range, are very realistic indeed.

Most importantly from the conservation point of view, many of today's synthetic corals look so authentic that they are contributing significantly to a decrease in the use of the traditional bleached coral skeletons that were once so popular with marine aquarists.

option: living rock. This consists of chunks of rock encrusted with, and bored by, seaweeds and invertebrates. Used judiciously, living rock can bring a degree of "instant maturity" to the appearance of an aquarium. More importantly, properly looked after rock will help to maintain water quality at the desired level. However, remember that an "instantly matured" look does not mean that maturity has actually been established. In fact, unless the living rock is in good condition and it is introduced into a well-balanced system, some of the organisms living on and in it will not survive long. If this happens, that initial look of maturity will be short-lived and will present serious problems with the quality of the water. It is therefore probably a better idea to introduce living rock into an already established aquarium than into a brand-new one.

Artificial rocks can be used to remarkably good effect, as in this tank of Wimplefish, also known as Poor Man's Moorish Idol

31

SETTING UP AN AQUARIUM: A STEP-BY-STEP GUIDE

There must be as many ways of setting up an aquarium as there are aquarists, and no two home aquariums can ever be exactly the same, even if their dimensions are identical. A few extra fish or plants, a little more (or less) gravel – the same numbers of fish, but in different sizes or in different male-to-female ratios, can all exert a major influence on conditions within an aquarium.

The actual location of the tank, the equipment chosen, the quality of the water you put in it, or any other one of a multitude of factors can result in two aquariums, which have been set up following the same sequence of steps, ending up with different levels of success.

If on reading this, you feel, as a potential aquarist, that the task is next to impossible, rest assured that this could not be further from the truth. Setting up a successful aquarium is not only possible, it is quite easy as well. The important thing to remember is that there are a few basic rules.

First, you must do your research thoroughly. Make sure that you consider as many of the pros and cons of the various options open to you as possible in terms of type of aquarium, species choice, equipment, finances and the time at your disposal to look after the system and its inhabitants properly once everything is set up.

Because the actual setting up should not present a major hurdle but be an enjoyable experience, this is usually not one of the main deciding factors when it comes to choosing the sector of the hobby to enter. Whether you decide on a freshwater, brackish or marine aquarium, the setting-up procedures share several common steps. A step-by-step guide to setting up an aquarium suitable for freshwater community species is given below. It is followed by additional or alternative steps for some of the other main types.

As we have noted, there is no one, single, foolproof method of setting up an aquarium. What therefore follows are steps that I have used and found successful over the years. However, do not regard them as constituting a rigid inflexible format. They are guidelines and, as such, have a degree of built-in flexibility.

If you have not yet fully decided whether to go for freshwater, brackish or marine tropicals, read this section through to see which setting-up procedures you are most comfortable with, and if you find that something strikes you as a little awkward or difficult to handle, you may want to go for an easier-sounding option and move on to a more awkward-sounding one after you have mastered the basics of running your first choice for a while.

FRESHWATER COMMUNITY AQUARIUM

Follow the step-by-step written sequence below, and the photographic sequence on the following pages.

STEP I

Check that you have bought all the necessary equipment: aquarium, stand (if necessary), hood (unnecessary if spotlights or mercury bulbs have been chosen), condensation tray, lights, starter unit (if lights are fluorescent), heater-stat, thermometer, aerator, air line, non-return valve, diffuser stone, filter, filter mediums (if model is not of the undergravel type), gravel, gravel pad (if desired), terracing/rocks/wood, plants (to be kept moist), plugs (one for each piece of electrical equipment, although if a cable tidy is used, only one plug may be necessary) and water-testing kits.

Certain items of accessory equipment, algae scrapers and nets will need to be bought soon, but are not absolutely essential on the first day.

STEP 2

Select a site away from direct sunlight, drafts and extremes of temperature. Check that the piece of furniture on which the tank will rest is strong enough (this does not, of course, apply if you are using a proper aquarium stand or cabinet). Water is very heavy – 8.3lb per gallon (4.5kg per 4.5 liters) – and rocks weigh even more.

STEP 3

Test the tank for leaks and repair them or exchange the tank if necessary.

STEP 4

Rest the empty tank on polystyrene strips or sheets.

STEP 5

Add the gravel, sand or other substrates in the following sequence:

- Place the undergravel filter in position, if one is being used.
- Lay gravel pad on top of the filter plates if one is being used.
- Insert the airlift tube into the filter base.
- Rinse gravel/sand thoroughly in a plastic bucket until the water runs clear.
- Spread a layer of gravel or sand on the filter plate or gravel pad.
- Add the layer or pockets of organic planting medium if required.
- Add the remainder of gravel/sand and arrange any rocks, bogwood, etc.

STEP 6

Place the heater/stat, air line and the internal filters in position, making sure that the base of the heating unit does not touch the gravel. **Do not switch anything on!**

STEP 7

Fill the aquarium with water, install the plants and setup the equipment. This is best done in the following sequence:

- Start filling the aquarium with water. Avoid disturbing the bedding medium by pouring the water onto a sheet of newspaper, greaseproof paper or plastic laid over the items in the base of the aquarium. Alternatively, pour the water into a jar placed on a saucer. The important thing is to avoid direct contact between the stream of water and the bedding medium.
- Fill the aquarium half full only.
- Add a small quantity of warm water to raise the temperature (even plants can feel the cold!).
- Remove the newspaper, jars and so forth.
- Introduce the plants, making sure that small subjects are placed near the front and that plants such as *Vallisneria*, whose leaves emerge from a crown, are planted so that the crowns are exposed, or they will rot.

- Add water conditioners and dechlorinator.
- Complete the filling process, leaving at least 1in (2.5cm) between the surface water and the top edge of the glass.
- Arrange the power filter inflow/outflow tubes, or push the powerhead into position on top of the undergravel filter airlift.
- Lower the condensation tray into position.
- Install lights in the hood.
- Place hood in its permanent position.
- Arrange the cables, air line, starter unit and so on in a hood compartment if this is available. If it is not, arrange the leads and the air line neatly out of view behind the aquarium by using, for example, a cable tidy.
- Insert nonreturn valve in the air line.
- Locate the aerator above tank level, suspending it, for example, from a hook on the wall.
- set up the power filter connections.

STEP 8

Start the aquarium running, following this sequence:

- Switch on all electrical equipment. Ideally this should be done early in the day to allow time for monitoring and making adjustments.
- Adjust air and filter flow rates, making sure that neither is too turbulent.
- Check the temperature hourly and adjust thermostat if necessary.

Warning: Switch off all electrical appliances before any adjustments are made, and allow heater to cool down for about 10 minutes before removing it from the water.

- Test pH and hardness and adjust if necessary.
- Run the system on a 12 to 15 hour light period for about a week if possible. Although this trial period is not absolutely necessary with the water treatments and conditioners available today, it is advisable, because it allows the aquarium to settle down and gives you an opportunity to carry out adjustments and generally become familiar with the art of aquarium management.

Blacktailed Humbug

STAGES OF THE STEP-BY-STEP SEQUENCE IN PICTURES

After choosing the correct location, and placing the tank on polystyrene strips or sheets, the undergravel filter is laid on the base of the tank

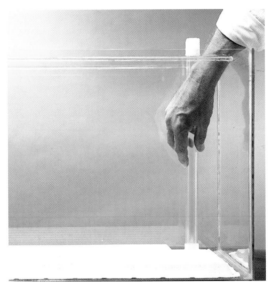

Inserting the airlift tube into the filter base

Washing the gravel

A layer of gravel is spread on the filter plate

Arranging the rocks

The heater/thermostat is placed in position, ensuring that the base of the unit does not touch the gravel. The airline and diffuser stone are inserted into the airlift tube. The tank is half-filled with water and the plants are positioned.

Nothing should be switched on at this stage

The tank is then filled to within 1in (2.5cm) of the top of the tank, and the positioning of plants readjusted if required

The condensation tray is lowered into position. This plastic sheeting will ensure that no condensation or splashed water will come into contact with the lighting elements

Lights are installed in the hood and all cables, the starter unit, etc., are arranged in the back of the hood

Gouramis in an established aquarium, provided with plenty of greenery

OTHER FRESHWATER AQUARIUMS

Generally speaking, the above guidelines may be followed, with minor modifications, for most freshwater systems. Should some of the species being considered require open midwater or surface space, such as shoaling tetras (midwater) or half-beaks (surface swimmers), this can be comfortably provided for. Similarly, if relatively high numbers of cave dwellers, like some cichlids, or species of catfish that like resting under logs during the day, are being considered, flowerpots, slates, inert rocks, bogwood and so on should be introduced.

One particular type of freshwater aquarium does, however, require special consideration. It is the African rift lake system. Fish from these areas require hard, alkaline conditions, and occur in quite high densities in the wild and many like to have numerous nooks, crannies and caves to hide in. Most also like to have clear swimming space and may require at least some open sandy areas. All of these features can be provided here, in a single aquarium, given a little thought, time and care.

These aquariums require very efficient filtration, largely because of the higher-than-normal stocking densities recommended (see Stocking Freshwater Aquariums on page 39) and the lack of plants. Power filters are, therefore, usually considered better choices than undergravel ones in these instances.

If a power filter is to be employed, neither the installation of an undergravel unit nor a gravel pad will apply. Instead, the gravel/coral sand mixture should be laid directly on the bottom pane of the aquarium. The rocks – and you will need plenty

of them – can be laid directly on the sand/gravel base or bedded well into it to prevent them from toppling over. It is easier to use large stones for the bottom layer, gradually decreasing their size as subsequent layers are added to create a back wall of rocks reaching up to the surface of the water. Such an arrangement provides the numerous caves and tunnels that many species prefer, as well as the open swimming space at the front where the fish can be viewed at their best, and a sandy/gravelly substratum for the diggers.

A further development of this overall theme involves the creation of adequately spaced territories for species that require these. Julies from Lake Tanganyika, for example, spawn on flat surfaces under cover and defend their personal

Colorful African rift lake cichlids

patch against intruders. Yet other African cichlids are shell dwellers and spawners. These tiny species therefore require the provision of empty snail shells appropriately spaced with open water and substratum between them to allow these fish to establish and defend their small territories without excessive levels of stress.

There are so many species of cichlids and other freshwater fish available today that the permutations with regard to particular requirements are virtually endless. It is therefore wise to study the species in advance and to seek advice from retailers and experienced aquarists, incorporating this information into the setting-up procedures and adapting the general guidelines described above to ensure maximum benefit all-round.

BRACKISH WATER AQUARIUMS

We have already referred to two types of brackish water aquariums: the mangrove swamp type and the "marine" brackish type. There are, of course, numerous intergradations between the two, but separating them in this way makes the concept a little more manageable. Clearly, aquariums containing even more freshwater than that found in the mangrove system are closer to the true freshwater types and are, in a sense, easier to manage. However, if you are a little unsure of tackling genuinely brackish conditions, you may decide that you want to start off with an "almost-freshwater" aquarium.

The disadvantage of such a choice, however, is that the resulting aquarium can end up more or less like a standard freshwater one, with relatively minor changes such as using driftwood instead of bogwood.

Mangrove Swamp Aquariums
The general setting-up procedures for a mangrove swamp aquarium are basically as outlined earlier for a freshwater community aquarium, but one of the main differences is that mangroves often harbor species of fish, such as mudskippers, that like to come out onto the mudbanks to feed. If you plan to keep mudskippers, therefore, the substratum, which could include some coral sand or gravel mixed in with normal gravel or silver sand, should be sloped in such a way that it provides a surface for grazing and resting. This will be impossible to achieve in a tank that is filled to within the customary inch or so of the top edge, so when you are filling the aquarium, the amount of water will be determined by the depth of gravel or other substratum that needs to be left exposed.

A further departure in the setting-up sequence is that marine salt needs to be mixed in with the water before it is added to the aquarium. The actual amount will depend on the level of salinity required. As a rough guide:

- 0.2oz marine salt/gallon (1.5gm/liter) will result in a specific gravity (SG) reading of around 1.0002, which is only slightly brackish.
- 1.03oz marine salt/gallon (8gm/liter) will result in an SG value of about 1.008.

Marine Brackish Aquariums
Once the level of salt added to the water begins to raise the specific gravity above about 1.010, it is probably reasonable to start looking at the setting up of such an aquarium more in line with the requirements usually associated with marine set-ups. The coral sand/gravel content of the substratum, for instance, should be higher than in the mangrove swamp system, and it gets closer to 100 percent the closer we get to genuine marine conditions.

At the highest salinites, few if any of the plants that could be accommodated within a mangrove-type aquarium will survive, and decorations such as driftwood can now either be replaced by, or used in conjunction with, more genuinely marine objects such as seashells and synthetic corals.

MARINE AQUARIUMS

There is no doubt that marine aquariums are more difficult than their freshwater or brackish equivalents. This does not make them impossible – just more challenging. The margin of error is also smaller, so your preparations must be that much more precise and thorough. Although the basic setting-up steps for marine aquariums are similar to those for a freshwater system, there are a few significant differences.

Laying the Substratum
The substratum will usually consist of two layers: a coarse layer of gravel or chips lying either directly on the base, or on top of the undergravel filter (if one is being used). This is covered with a gravel pad, which is topped with finer material like coral sand.

Choosing the Rockwork
The rockwork can be of similar composition, and be arranged in similar ways to those in African rift lake systems. However, marine aquariums can also incorporate other materials, notably bleached, natural coral skeletons, which are now largely frowned upon, or synthetic ones. Wood is usually considered inappropriate, but fossil or petrified wood can be used.

Inert but attractive rocks, including natural and synthetic lava rock and the like, can also be incorporated. Living rock is not considered a good choice for aquariums that will be dedicated exclusively to fish, because these will usually make a meal of any invertebrates contained within the rock as soon as they poke out their heads, feet or tentacles or venture out in search of food.

A fine example of a well-established marine aquarium

Filling the Aquarium

Although the actual filling process itself is similar in both freshwater and marine aquariums, some additional "pre-filling" stages must be observed in marine aquariums. First calculate the volume of the aquarium. This is done by multiplying the length by the breadth by the depth. If you measure these in inches and divide the total by 242.5 you will have the total volume in gallons. For example, a tank measuring 40 x 18 x 12in will hold:

$$\frac{40 \times 18 \times 12}{242.5} = \frac{8640}{242.5} = 35.6 \text{ gallons}$$

This is the total volume. The actual furnished volume – that is, when all the rocks, gravel and so on are in place – will be between 80 and 90 percent of this, depending on the amount of rocks and gravel used. This will work out at between 28 – 32 gallons, which will come to approximately 108 – 121 liters. Approximations will be quite adequate at this stage.

Having worked out these figures to the nearest gallon or so, choose one or other of the two following procedures to dissolve the required amount of salt in the water.

● **Aquarium method**: Fill the aquarium to within 2in (5cm) or so of the eventual water level, having first allowed the water to run for a few minutes (particularly if you are doing this in the morning) so that any potentially toxic chemicals, such as copper or lead that might be present in the water supply pipes, are eliminated. Follow the directions given on the packet of marine salt. Dissolve enough salt in this water to give a specific gravity reading on the hydrometer that falls within the desired range of 1.021 and 1.024. If you prefer, the salt can be added to the aquarium before it is filled.

● **Bucket method:** Mix a small but known volume of water and marine salt, measuring the SG with the hydrometer before adding the solution to the aquarium. Repeat this procedure until the aquarium has been filled to the desired level. *Note:* Do not use metal buckets, and mix the salt with a wooden or plastic utensil.

Allow the salt to dissolve completely and then, once the temperature has been allowed to rise to its required level, check the SG again and adjust, either with freshwater or a salt mix as necessary. Complete the filling-up process if no further rockwork is being added. If living rock is to be included a little later, either fill up the tank at this stage and then drain away the required amount when the rock is introduced, or simply leave the water level as it is and adjust it later if necessary.

STOCKING AND MAINTAINING AN AQUARIUM

The nature of the environment within an aquarium begins to change and mature as soon as the setting-up procedures have been completed. A newly set-up system is, however, far too "raw" to accept any animals, although plants may be able to cope better. A period of maturation is required for all aquariums, and even though water conditioners and maturing agents will speed things up considerably, problems will undoubtedly arise if the process is pushed beyond certain limits. So common are these problems, in fact, that there is a collective term for them: New Tank Syndrome.

These problems can be avoided by following a few basic rules, and in freshwater aquariums the initial maturation stages can successfully be negotiated in about a week, although marine systems take considerably longer.

Freshwater Aquariums
Run the aquarium on a 12 to 15 hour illumination period for about a week, adjusting the temperature and so on as required. During this time, the water may become cloudy, but this is quite normal. It will clear in a few days as the biological activity of the filter gets into gear. Although the full complement of plants can be installed from the very beginning, no fish should be added until this maturation stage is over.

Marine Aquariums
Run the aquarium as for a freshwater system, but the addition of a maturing agent in a marine aquarium is strongly recommended. Do not, however, add any hardy fish. This is both unnecessary and unfair to these unfortunate "guinea pigs," which may, if they survive, establish their own territories, making later introductions difficult.

As the aquarium matures, it will go through what is known as the nitrite crisis. Depending on the temperature and bacterial population, this process will take about a month or even a little longer. Even after this time, the filter will be too immature to handle heavy loads, so stocking must be done very carefully. In fact, it will take up to a year for a marine tank to be able to handle its full complement of fish.

Choosing Fish and Invertebrates
However careful you are, you can never be 100 percent certain of selecting healthy fish, and when it comes to invertebrates, it is even more difficult. Nevertheless, following a few general rules will help reduce the risks considerably.

● Buy quarantined (acclimatized) stocks. Failing this – or in addition to it – acclimatize all new stock for about a week in a separate aquarium. If the stocks you are buying are the first, your new, but partially matured, aquarium will serve as appropriate quarters.

● Buy only fish that are lively and well colored for their species, that hold their fins erect, that are full-bodied and that are known to be feeding. You must familiarize yourself with the characteristics of the species in advance so that you know what constitutes "normal" color and behavior. If you are buying invertebrates, check even more

thoroughly because many species will give only subtle clues about their condition.

● If there are any dead or obviously ill fish or invertebrates in the shop tank from which you are planning to make a choice, resist the temptation to buy, even if the fish or invertebrate you want to buy looks as if it is overflowing with health.

● If at all possible, buy your stocks late in the afternoon so that by the time you get home it is early evening and you can introduce them to your aquarium at a time that avoids the additional stresses that all the daytime activities around the tank can generate.

Rummy-nosed Tetras and Cardinals in a heavily stocked tank

Stocking
There are so many different kinds of aquarium fish and their requirements differ so widely that it is quite impossible to give universally applicable, foolproof figures concerning the numbers of fish that an aquarium will hold. Even the same aquarium will vary in the number of fish of a single species that it can accommodate if the temperature, diet, filtration, aeration or any other factor is altered.

Stocking Freshwater Aquariums
It is essential not to be too ambitious, particularly at the outset. A safe way to stock a freshwater tropical aquarium is to start off at the 50 percent level and to add fish gradually over a period of weeks. This approach has the added advantage that it avoids stretching the biological capacity of a filter beyond its limits, thus giving it time to mature and to enhance its efficiency in tune with the slowly increasing fish population.

The figures given in the table on page 40 represent approximate stocking levels (at full capacity)

APPROXIMATE RECOMMENDED STOCKING LEVELS (FRESHWATER AQUARIA)

Aquarium surface in in/cm (approximate dimensions)		Number of fish, organized by size		
		Up to 2in (5cm)	2–3in (5–7.5cm)	3–4in (7.5–10cm)
18 x 10in	45 x 25cm	14	10	not recommended
24 x 12in	60 x 30cm	22	16	14
36 x 12in	90 x 30cm	33	24	21
46 x 12in	120 x 30cm	44	32	29
60 x 18in	150 x 45cm	83	60	54

for fish that are neither overaggressive nor possess other undesirable qualities that dictate that they should be kept either individually or in pairs. Note that the sizes of the fish are measured in body length: the length of the tail is not included.

If you are stocking a tank of African rift lake cichlid species, increase the suggested levels by about 50 percent. This crowding tends to "spread out" the aggression, thus reducing the risks of any individual becoming the focus of concerted attack. As previously mentioned, such tanks do, however, require efficient filtration.

Stocking Marine Aquariums

Because the maturation period must be longer, and because of other factors, such as the lower oxygen-carrying capacity of seawater and the higher toxicity of contaminants like ammonia, stocking levels are lower in marine aquariums. Ideally, the full carrying capacity of a marine aquarium should not be achieved until the filter is about a year old.

While it is traditional to calculate stocking levels for freshwater aquariums in inches/centimeters per unit of surface area, marine aquariums have (equally traditionally) been treated in terms

Transport fish within a heat-resistant box

of inches/centimeters per unit volume. A further difference is that although the full stocking level can be established within a few weeks in freshwater systems, marine equivalents are dealt with in two stages:

● During the first six months (once the trial maturation stage has been completed) stocking should be carried on gradually to achieve an eventual density of 1in (2.5cm) of fish (discounting tail) per 4.8 gallons (18 liters) of water.

● During the second six months this stocking level can be gradually increased to 1in (2.5cm) per 2.4 gallons (9 liters) of water.

Depending on the species and their requirements, invertebrates can generally be stocked at higher densities, but even so, the buildup must be gradual to ensure that the filter can cope with the increasing load.

Introducing Specimens

There are various ways in which specimens can be successfully introduced. The following steps are generally regarded as those that will offer a safe method of introducing specimens into an aquarium, but as with other techniques, there can be some flexibility. For instance, some aquarists never release the water in the transportation bag into the aquarium when they transfer the fish or invertebrates, while others invariably do so.

Two key factors that all introduction techniques share are the gradual matching of the conditions of the "transportation" water to those of the aquarium and the minimizing of stress for the stock.

● Minimize any possible heat loss on the way home by ensuring that the packed fish are placed in a heat-resistant bag, such as those used to keep take-out food warm, or a box. Failing this, the bags containing the fish may be wrapped in newspaper or other insulating material. Avoid carrying exposed bags of fish – they are under enough stress already and can do without being subjected to this added ordeal.

Introducing the new specimens to the tank

● When you reach home, switch off the aquarium lights.

● Float the bags containing the fish or invertebrates in the aquarium.

● Leave the bags for about 10 minutes to allow the temperature to equalize. Individual bags may require a longer period if they contain a large volume of water.

● Untie the bags.

● Replace about a quarter of the water in each bag with aquarium water.

● Leave for 10 minutes.

● Repeat the two previous steps twice more, thereby introducing the animals to their new water chemistry gradually and helping to reduce environmental shock.

● Gently release the specimens into the aquarium.

● Leave the aquarium lights switched off.

● Do not feed the fish for several hours at least, and preferably not until the following morning.

If the above steps are carried out during the late afternoon or early evening, the fish and mobile invertebrates will have time to become accustomed to their new surroundings in natural fading light. They will be able to explore the aquarium and find suitable shelters for the night without having to do so in the full glare of the aquarium lights. They should also be allowed to see their first day in with naturally increasing daylight.

Feeding

The subject of diets and feeding is so vast that attempting to tackle it comprehensively here would be a futile task. Fortunately, most fish and many invertebrates fall within fairly broad categories, and the majority will readily take commercially prepared foods. Indeed, if you are a beginner, you should seriously consider avoiding species that do not take such foods readily. It is far better to learn how to keep easy-to-feed species successfully, and then move on to more challenging ones, than to start off with challenging subjects and fail. To do so would be to disregard one of the major basic responsibilities of all aquarists. You must, therefore, check in advance on the dietary needs of the fish and invertebrates that you intend to buy, and then buy only those that you can care for.

Some invertebrates require no feeding at all, as long as the light requirements are adequately met so that the symbiotic algae they contain can photosynthesize. To feed such organisms may, in fact, be completely pointless and lead to serious problems with water conditions. Others will require feeding only every few days, others need feeding once a week and so on.

As a general rule feed once or twice a day with only as much food of the correct type as can be cleared up in about 5 minutes. Any leftover food must be removed to prevent water pollution problems.

It cannot be said too often, however, that the specific needs of a species must be checked in advance. If in doubt, do not feed and seek immediate advice.

In properly stocked aquariums, a balance is achieved between plants and fish/invertebrates

AQUARIUM MAINTENANCE

Aquarium maintenance routines vary almost as much as setting-up procedures, and they must be tailored to the needs of the inhabitants of the aquarium and your own circumstances. However, some basic guidelines should be followed, which can be adapted as appropriate.

Daily Duties

● Feed fish at least twice if they are active shoalers or other types with high energy requirements. Adapt the frequency to suit other kinds of fish and invertebrates.

● Check on the state of health of aquarium inhabitants and remove affected individuals for treatment if necessary.

● Check for signs of breeding activity and remove fry or courting fish to appropriate quarters.

● Check the temperature of the water.

● Switch the aquarium lights on several minutes after the room lights have been on or after daybreak.

● Check the state of health of nocturnal and/or crepuscular (twilight) species in the evening and provide food for them just before, or just after, lights out.

● Switch the aquarium lights off several minutes before the room lights are switched off or shortly before natural daylight fades.

Weekly Duties

● Do not feed the fish for a day (this does not apply either to fish being conditioned for spawning or to fry and juveniles).

● Check heaters and thermostats for signs of faults such as leakages.

● Check the pH, hardness, specific gravity (marines), ammonia and nitrite levels of the water and take remedial action if necessary. Make sure that changes are made gradually.

● Check on your supplies of food, water treatments and remedies.

Every Other Week Duties

● Switch off the aeration (this does not apply to marine tanks).

● Gently rake or otherwise stir up the surface of the bedding medium.

● Scrape excess algal growth from the front of the aquarium.

● Allow the debris to settle.

● Siphon off the debris, together with 20–25 percent of the aquarium water.

● Replace this with fresh water whose temperature, pH and hardness and salinity, if appropriate, match conditions in the aquarium. If a larger volume of water is being replaced, the fresh water must be treated with a dechlorinator and/or dechloraminator.

● Switch on the aeration (this does not apply to marine systems).

Note: These regular partial water changes should not be carried out in the morning unless the water has been allowed to run for several minutes to eliminate toxic metallic ions such as copper. For marine aquariums, the interval can usually be extended to 3 to 4 weeks. If topping-up is required at any time, use freshwater, even for marine aquariums.

Every Third Week Duties

● Clean or replace nonbiological filter mediums in sponge/foam, canister-type or box filters.

● Rinse biological filter mediums in sponge/foam, canister-type or box-filters using aquarium water.

Note: Do not sterilize or boil biological mediums, because this will destroy their microfauna and, consequently, make them ineffective until a new population is established.

● If undergravel filtration is used, remove the air line from its airlift and scrape off any algal or calcite (hard water) deposits from the opening.

● Introduce a siphon tube down each undergravel filter airlift and suck out a small amount of accumulated mulm (organic debris) from under the filter plates.

● Clean or scrape diffuser stones.

● Check aerator diaphragms.

● Clean the nonreturn valve on the air line.

● Clean the condensation tray or cover glass.

● Check all lighting equipment – such as terminals.

● Remove any dead and dying leaves from plants, and prune, thin out and generally tidy up the vegetation.

● Replace poor plant specimens.

HEALTH

To many aquarists health is synonymous with disease, but this should not, in fact, be the case. Setting up a health-care program is a positive, preventive, proactive step, but setting up a disease-treatment program is a remedial, reactive measure. The fact is that the vast majority of health problems can be avoided by giving due attention to water quality, stocking and maintenance routines. Look after the water, and the water will look after your fish.

Adopting a health-conscious approach to keeping an aquarium is just as desirable as adopting a health-conscious approach to life. Both approaches reflect a positive attitude that is focused on preventing problems from arising in the first place. Other, more negative approaches tend to disregard the rules but then to depend on remedy-based measures that are stressful, both to the fish or invertebrates and to the aquarist.

Despite your best efforts, however, your stock could suffer from disease. When problems arise, never dose the aquarium with the first remedy that comes to hand. This is a sure and certain route to disaster. The first thing to do is carry out a thorough check of the water and other conditions to make sure that they are not causing the problem. Rectify any imbalances if appropriate.

As a new aquarist, you are not likely to be equipped, either in terms of experience or remedies, to deal with the more complex and serious fish diseases. Fortunately, help is never far away. A vet conversant in matters of fish health, staff, experienced aquarists and members of your local fish club will all be able to help you out. This is not to say that there are no diseases that a new aquarist can neither recognize nor treat. Those that do fall into this category are listed in the table below. However, there are many others that are difficult to diagnose without adequate equipment, materials or expertise. Some diseases require antibiotic treatment, and these compounds are not freely available over the counter in certain countries. In such cases, even if you are able to diagnose a particular disease accurately, you will still need a prescription from a vet to treat the problem.

COMMON FISH DISEASES AND TREATMENTS

FRESHWATER

Disease	Some symptoms	Some treatments
White spot or ich *Ichthyophthirius multifiliis*	Small white spots on body and fins; fish may scratch constantly	Many proprietary (brand-name) treatments are available
Slime disease *Ichthyobodo, Trichodina, Chilodonella*	Shiny/blue-white coloration on skin; excessive production of mucus	White spot remedies may work; if not, a commercial anti-parasite remedy should be tried
Gill fluke infection *Dactylogyrus*	Excessive mucus; inflamed gills; fast breathing rate; scratching of gill covers	Proprietary treatments are available
Skin fluke infection *Gyrodactylus*	Inflamed skin patches; erratic swimming; excessive mucus production; scratching	Same as for gill fluke infection

White spot disease

Slime disease showing as shiny white areas

White patches of fungus

Velvet disease showing as multiple spots

Neon Tetra suffering from dropsy

Ulceration on the flanks

Fungus or cottonwool disease *Saprolegnia*	Fluffy, whitish patches on body or fins	Proprietary treatments are available
Velvet *Piscinoodinium*	Whitish or rust-colored "dusting" of very fine spots on body and fins	Proprietary treatments are available
Anchor worm *Lernaea*	Slim, white wormlike parasites attached to body or fins, usually with two white "appendages" (egg sacs)	Some proprietary treatments are available; removal of the parasites with a fine pair of forceps may also be necessary
Bacterial infections *Aeromonas* and others	Blood spots or patches; open wounds; ulceration; frayed fins; dropsy (swollen abdomen, with scales sticking out)	Such diseases require antibiotic treatment. Seek advice (and prescription) from a vet
Mouth fungus *Flexibacter*	White growth around the mouth; jawbones may be eroded	Some proprietary treatments are available. (Do not use "normal" fungus remedy as this disease is bacterial in nature)

MARINE*

Disease	**Some symptoms**	**Some treatments**
Marine white spot *Cryptocaryon*	Similar to freshwater white spot	Freshwater bath (but be very careful not to overstress the patient), followed by copper-based treatment, but not in invertebrate aquaria
Marine velvet *Amyloodinium*	Similar to freshwater velvet	Copper-based treatment, plus short freshwater baths

Marine white spot on a Gray Mullet

Marine white spot on an Achilles Tang

* In addition to marine white spot and marine velvet, which are specific to marine fish, marine fish are prone to other diseases whose symptoms and treatment are similar to those listed for freshwater species, most notably bacterial and skin parasite infections. Copper is a very effective treatment against many diseases of marine fish. However, it is lethal to invertebrates and must therefore not be used in aquariums housing such creatures.

Freshwater baths are very stressful for marine organisms. They often work because they kill off marine parasites through osmotic "shock," but a very careful watch must be kept on the fish being treated and the treatment must be stopped as soon as signs of stress (such as loss of balance) are spotted. The presence of an experienced observer/assistant who has carried out such procedures before will be found invaluable by first-time practitioners.

PART 3
THE SPECIES

THE SPECIES

Previous page:
**A beautiful shoal of
Leopard Danios**

The range of fish, plants and invertebrates that is now available runs into thousands of species and varieties. All have desirable characteristics in one way or another and many are so endearing that it is hard to resist them. Yet not all are suitable for new aquarists, either because of their eventual size, aggressive habits or voracious appetites, or because they are difficult to keep. Two outstanding examples are piranha, on the freshwater side, and seahorses on the marine side. The former have a reputation that speaks for itself (although their killer qualities are grossly overexaggerated), while the latter, although widely available, are challenging, even for many experienced aquarists.

In the pages that follow, you will find a wide selection of species, some of which, in any terms, must be regarded as difficult to keep. They are, however, available in shops and they may therefore tempt many first-time aquarists. Despite their availability, it would be a grave error to buy these species until some experience has been gained with hardier and easier types. They are included to inform potential buyers about some of their demanding requirements and thus, hopefully, to discourage newcomers to the hobby from including them in an initial shopping list, and to delay buying them until they are more familiar with the skills required for effective aquarium husbandry.

Common or scientific names?

There are over 20,000 species of fish and many more invertebrates. The vast majority have officially documented scientific names. The small minority that do not have such a name, will, in due course, have one. Many species also have a common name, which is usually considerably easier to pronounce and remember than the scientific equivalent, and you may wonder why we do not dispense with scientific names altogether and stick to more manageable common ones.

There are several reasons. For a start, scientific names are recognized the world over, whereas an English or Italian common name will mean little or nothing to someone who does not speak that language. In addition, a particular species can often be known by different common names, even within a single country. For example, Medakas, Rice Fish and Geisha Girls are not three distinct fish, but one, scientifically known as *Oryzias latipes*.

Conversely, the same common name may be used to refer to different fish. For instance, if someone speaks of a Mosquito Fish, he or she could be referring to the species known scientifically as *Heterandria formosa*, or to one or other of two *Gambusia* species, *Gambusia affinis* or *Gambusia holbrooki*. In addition, there are many species that, quite simply, do not have a common name at all, so they cannot be referred to by one even if we wanted to.

The Species Guide

The "traditional" method of discussing fish, invertebrates and plants is to group them as freshwater, brackish and marine species. However, because the aim of this book is to provide an easy-to-follow guide for potential aquarists who have no experience with the hobby, the species guide has been divided as follows:

● **Recommended species for beginners**, which is further broken down into freshwater tropical species, "coldwater" tropical species, brackish water species and marine species of fish and invertebrates. So many species fall in this category that it will be possible to feature only a representative selection.

● **Second-level species** are more difficult to keep, and this section therefore includes general advice regarding these species, and cites some of the most common/notable examples.

● **Species for experienced aquarists** are discussed in general terms and this section includes some of the more widely encountered species that beginners might feel tempted to buy but should not.

● **Plants** are listed in three sections: freshwater species, brackish water species and marine species. There are numerous freshwater plants available these days, but very few brackish or marine ones, a fact that is reflected in the selection.

SPECIES FOR BEGINNERS

FRESHWATER SPECIES

The following table includes some of the most widely available species. These are generally referred to as "community fish" because of the relative ease with which they can be kept and bred in aquariums, their compatibility, their reasonable price and their beauty.

In addition to the species listed here, all of which have individual entries on the following pages, a selection of other species and varieties appear in this section in summary tables. Even then, only a representative sample of the fish that are actually available can be considered, so ask for advice from your aquatic shop or from an experienced aquarist. You may well find other equally beautiful and suitable species among the several thousands available.

Common name	Scientific name	Comments
LIVEBEARERS Family: **Poeciliidae** Molly	*Poecilia latipinna;* *P. sphenops; P. velifera*	Mollies should be kept in water containing I teaspoonful of salt per 1.2 gallons (4.5 liters).
Guppy	*Poecilia reticulata*	Numerous fancy varieties available.
Swordtail; Platy	*Xiphophorus helleri;* *X. maculatus, X. variatus*	Species are closely related and will interbreed.
EGGLAYERS Family: **Belontiidae** Siamese Fighter	*Betta splendens*	Only single males to be kept safely in a community aquarium.
Dwarf Gourami; Two or Three-spot/ Blue/Opaline (Cosby)/ Golden/Platinum Gourami	*Colisa lalia; Trichogaster* *trichopterus*	These species have special air-breathing organs. *T. trichopterus* males can be aggressive.
Family: **Callichthyidae** Bronze Corydoras	*Corydoras aeneus*	A sturdy bottom-level feeder.
Family: **Characidae** Black Widow	*Gymnocorymbus ternetzi*	Attractive shoaler.
Rummy-nosed Tetras	*Hemigrammus rhodostomus*	Slim-bodied with distinctive red head.
Neon Tetra; Cardinal Tetra	*Paracheirodon innesi;* *P. axelrodi*	These two species are very similar, but Cardinal Tetras have more color. Both are shoalers.
Family: **Cichlidae** Angelfish	*Pterophyllum scalare*	Only small specimens should be kept in a community tank.
Kribensis	*Pelvicachromis pulcher*	Females more colorful than males.
Family: **Cobitidae** Kuhli Loach	*Acanthophthalmus* spp.	This is a peaceful, eel-like species.
Family: **Cypridinae** Tiger Barb	*Barbus tetrazona*	A lively shoaling species. May nip fins.
Zebra Danio	*Brachydanio rerio*	A very fast-swimming shoaler.
Flying Fox	*Epalzeorhynchus kallopterus*	Torpedo-shaped, fast-swimmer.
Harlequin	*Rasbora heteromorpha*	Shoaling species with a dark, cone-shaped patch in the posterior half of the body.
Family: **Gyrinocheilidae** Chinese Algae Eater/ Sucking Loach	*Gyrinocheilus aymonieri*	A sucker-mouthed, fast-swimming herbivore. Some can be aggressive.
Family: **Loricariidae** Plecostomus	*Hypostomus* spp.	A sucker-mouthed herbivore.

LIVEBEARERS

Family: **Poeciliidae**

According to most modern thinking, this family consists of three subfamilies, two of which are egglayers and one, the Poeciliinae (which is the one we are interested in here), made up of livebearers.
As their name implies, instead of laying eggs as most fish do, livebearers give birth to fully formed young.

SAILFIN MOLLY
Poecilia latipinna, P. velifera

These species are superficially similar, but *P. velifera*, which is also, more correctly, known as the Yucatan Molly, is considerably larger. In wild populations of *P. latipinna* not all males develop the characteristic sailfin. Both species have been crossbred and many of the aquarium varieties have arisen as a result.

SPECIES DETAILS
Size: *P. latipinna*: males around 4in (10cm); females 4³/₄in (12cm)
P. velifera: males up to 6in (15cm); females 7in (18cm)

Origin: *P. latipinna*: Carolina, Virginia, Texas, Florida and the Atlantic coast of Mexico; *P. velifera*: Yucatan Peninsula of Mexico
Ease of keeping: Moderately easy
Breeding: Large broods (up to 140 fry) every 6–10 weeks are not uncommon

AQUARIUM CARE
Water: Alkaline, medium-hard water containing 5–10 percent seawater/salt preferred
Temperature: 23°–28°C (73°–82°F), with the higher end being better for long-term health and breeding
Food: A wide range of commercial foods accepted; should contain a vegetable complement

GUPPY
Poecilia reticulata

Also known as the Millions Fish, the Guppy is a species in which the tiny, infinitely variable males are more colorful than the females. In recent years, nicely colored females have also been developed, and these are fast

becoming popular in their own right. In the wild, the Guppy has short fins. In cultivated forms, however, the tail (caudal) fin, in particular, has been developed into numerous shapes and sizes. New varieties of Guppy are appearing every year.

SPECIES DETAILS
Size: Wild males to about 1¹/₄in (3cm); females to 2in (5cm). Cultivated forms grow considerably larger than this
Origin: Occurs widely north of the Amazon and has been introduced into many countries over the years, largely as a biological control of the mosquito
Ease of keeping: Easy
Breeding: Broods of about 50 fry are produced every 4–6 weeks by medium-sized females

AQUARIUM CARE
Water: Medium hard
Temperature: This is a tough little fish, which will withstand a wide range of conditions but prefers temperatures between 70°–77°F (21°–25°C)
Food: Eats all commercial foods

Guppy

Sailfin Molly

Sphenops Molly

BLACK MOLLY/ SPHENOPS MOLLY
Poecilia sphenops

Traditionally, the Black Molly (as distinct from the Black Sailfin Molly) has been referred to as *P. sphenops*. Recent research suggests that the short-finned Black Molly developed from a cross between a black form of Sailfin *P. latipinna* and a genuine Sphenops Molly (*P. sphenops*). But, whatever their origins, the Black Molly and the Sphenops Molly are attractive and popular fish.

SPECIES DETAILS
Size: Wild populations: males around 2¼ in (6cm); females 3¼ in (8cm)
Origin: The genuine wild (green) Sphenops Molly occurs from Texas down through Mexico (along the coasts) to Colombia

Black Sphenops Molly

Ease of keeping: Moderately easy
Breeding: Around 80 fry every 5 – 7 weeks

AQUARIUM CARE
Water: Alkaline, medium-hard water containing 5–10 percent seawater/salt preferred
Temperature: 73°–82°F (23°–28°C), with the higher end being better for long-term health and breeding
Food: A wide range of commercial foods accepted; should contain a vegetable complement

SWORDTAIL
Xiphophorus helleri

A highly distinctive species, in which the lower rays of the tail (caudal) fin of the slim-bodied, fast-swimming males extend into the characteristic "sword." There are numerous forms in the wild and a huge and ever-expanding range of commercially produced varieties. It is an active, hardy fish, but because males dislike each other, it is advisable to keep a single male in an aquarium. Females do not share this characteristic. Most aquarium swordtails have platy genes in their makeup.

SPECIES DETAILS
Size: Males: to 5½ in (14cm) excluding the sword; females to 6¼ in (16cm). However,

Male Hi-fin Swordtail

Female Gold Swordtail

some commercial varieties are considerably smaller than this

Origin: Atlantic littoral, from Veracruz, Mexico, to northern Honduras. Also introduced into many localities outside its natural range, including Sri Lanka and Australia
Ease of keeping: Easy
Breeding: Large broods of up to 50 fry will be produced every 4– 6 weeks

AQUARIUM CARE
Water: Tolerant of a wide range of aquarium conditions, but not poor water quality
Temperature: Between 72°–79°F (22°–26°C)
Food: Will accept a wide range of commercial foods

Southern Platies

Short-finned Sunset Platy

SOUTHERN PLATY
Xiphophorus maculatus

The Southern Platy or Moonfish is usually referred to simply as the Platy. As with the Guppy, wild populations are variable in coloration.

SPECIES DETAILS
Size: Males: around 1¹/₂ in (4cm); females to 2¹/₂ in (6cm). These figures are highly variable
Origin: Atlantic littoral from Veracruz, Mexico, southward to British Honduras, Belize and Guatemala. Also introduced into numerous localities outside its range, including Nigeria and Saudi Arabia
Ease of keeping: Moderately easy

Breeding: Fry are produced in batches of 40–50 every 4–6 weeks

AQUARIUM CARE
Water: It will tolerate a wide range of conditions, but this does not include substandard water quality. Well-planted aquariums suit it best
Temperature: 68°–79°F (20°–26°C), preferably toward the higher end of the range
Food: A wide range of foods will be accepted
Special needs: Well-planted aquariums

SUNSET PLATY
Xiphophorus variatus

This delightful species has several other common names:
Variable, Variatus, Variegated or (rarely) Moctezuma Platy. Like its closest relatives, and the Guppy, it occurs in different forms in the wild. It will also hybridize easily with the Southern Platy and Swordtail.

SPECIES DETAILS
Size: Wild males: to 1³/₄ in (4.5cm); females around 2¹/₈ in (5.5cm) but often larger. Commercial varieties can grow larger still
Origin: The Atlantic slope of Mexico, but introduced into several locations outside its natural range
Ease of keeping: Easy
Breeding: Fry (around 50, but up to 100) will be produced every 4–6 weeks

AQUARIUM CARE
Water: Will tolerate a wide range of conditions, but slightly alkaline/hard water is preferred
Temperature: As low as 61°F (16°C) has been recorded at collecting sites in the wild, but 68°–81°F (20°–27°C) is optimal
Food: A wide variety of commercial foods accepted

Hi-fin Sunset Platy

EGGLAYERS

Family: **Belontiidae**

SIAMESE FIGHTER
Betta splendens

This beautiful fish has been developed into many spectacularly colored, long-finned varieties. Despite the pugnacious name, only males are aggressive, and then only toward other males of the same species. The females, all of which are short-finned, are generally placid and retiring.

SPECIES DETAILS
Size: Around 2$^1\!/_2$ in (6.5cm)
Origin: Mainly Thailand and Cambodia
Ease of keeping: Easy
Breeding: Eggs are laid in a bubble-nest, built and guarded by the male. Breeding will often occur in community aquariums. The male's aggression can cause a few problems at this time

AQUARIUM CARE
Water: Water chemistry is not critical
Temperature: Range should be 75°–86°F (24°–30°C)
Food: All commercial foods

DWARF GOURAMI
Colisa lalia

This is a great favorite for the community aquarium, and it is available in several color varieties, including Neon and Sunset and, more recently, as a long-finned variant. Males are much more colorful than females and become territorial during spawning.

SPECIES DETAILS
Size: Males: around 2in (5cm); females (and wild

specimens of both sexes): usually smaller
Origin: India, particularly Assam and Bengal
Ease of keeping: Easy
Breeding: Eggs laid in a bubble-nest, built and guarded by the male. Breeding often occurs in community aquariums, where the male's aggression at this time can cause a few problems

AQUARIUM CARE
Water: A wide range of conditions are tolerated
Temperature: 75°–82°F (24°–28°C)
Food: All commercial foods are accepted

Siamese Fighter

Sunset Dwarf Gourami

Neon Dwarf Gourami

Opaline Gouramis

TWO OR THREE-SPOT GOURAMI, BLUE GOURAMI, OPALINE (COSBY) GOURAMI, GOLDEN GOURAMI, PLATINUM GOURAMI
Trichogaster trichopterus

In addition to the above, other color varieties of this popular fish appear from time to time. Occasionally, even the true wild type, usually referred to as the Lavender or Brown Gourami, becomes available.

SPECIES DETAILS
Size: Up to 6in (15cm) but usually smaller, although males (which have fuller and more pointed dorsal and anal fins) are generally slimmer and slightly longer than females
Origin: Southeast Asia
Ease of keeping: Moderately easy
Breeding: Eggs are laid in a bubble-nest, built and guarded by the male. Breeding will often occur in community aquariums, where the male's aggression at this time can cause a few problems

AQUARIUM CARE
Water: Wide range of conditions tolerated.
Temperature: 73°–82°F (23°–28°C).
Food: Will take all commercial foods.

Honey Gourami

OTHER GOURAMIS
The term "Gourami" includes some species that are totally unsuitable for beginners, like the Giant Gourami (*Osphronemus goramy*) and the demanding Chocolate Gourami (*Sphaerichthys* spp.) and Licorice Gourami (*Parosphromenus* spp.), and the less delicate, but still somewhat challenging, *Trichopsis* species. The following are more tolerant of "community" conditions, but note the large size that some can attain.

Common name	Scientific name	Size
Honey Gourami	*Colisa sota*	2in/5cm
Indian/Striped/Giant Gourami	*Colisa fasciata*	4in/10cm
Thick-lipped Gourami	*Colisa labiosa*	3¼in/8cm
Kissing Gourami	*Helostoma temmincki*	12in/30cm
Pearl/Leeri/Lace Gourami	*Trichogaster leeri*	4in/10cm
Moonlight/Thin-lipped Gourami	*Trichogaster microlepis*	6in/15cm
Snakeskin Gourami	*Trichogaster pectoralis*	10in/25cm

Bronze Corydoras

Family: **Callichthyidae**

BRONZE CORYDORAS
Corydoras aeneus

This sturdy, attractive, bottom-dweller has sometimes (quite wrongly) been used as a scavenger, which will mop up the leftovers of any meal offered to the other tank inhabitants. Several varieties are now available, the most common being the albino, followed by rust- or orange-colored varieties.

SPECIES DETAILS
Size: About 3in (7.5cm)
Origin: Throughout South America
Ease of keeping: Easy
Breeding: Fertilized eggs are carried by the female between her cupped pelvic fins and deposited on plants and other surfaces

AQUARIUM CARE
Water: Will tolerate a wide range of conditions
Temperature: Should be 64°–79°F (18°–26°C)
Food: Will take all foods, particularly if they are fast-sinking types, such as food tablets

Family: **Characidae**

BLACK WIDOW
Gymnocorymbus ternetzi

Less streamlined than many other tetras, but it is an attractive shoaler, which has been developed into a number of fin and color variations, including a red morph.

SPECIES DETAILS
Size: Wild type: around 2in (5cm); farm-bred, long-finned varieties may be larger

Origin: Central South America
Ease of keeping: Easy
Breeding: An egg scatterer, which is unlikely to spawn in community aquariums

AQUARIUM CARE
Water: As long as untreated tapwater is avoided, this species is reasonably tolerant of water conditions
Temperature: 75°–82°F (24°–28°C)
Food: It will accept a wide range of commercial foods
Special Needs: Areas of clear surface water, as species sticks to upper reaches of water column

Long-finned Black Widow

OTHER CORYDORAS AND RELATED SPECIES
There are many species to choose from and more are being described all the time. All require the same general conditions.

Common name	Scientific name	Size
Britski's Catfish	*Brochis britskii*	4in/10cm
Emerald Catfish	*Brochis splendens*	4in/10cm
Blacktop Corydoras	*Corydoras acutus*	2¹⁄₈in/5.5cm
Arched, Skunk or Tabatinga Corydoras	*Corydoras arcuatus*	2in/5cm
Elegant Corydoras	*Corydoras elegans*	2¹⁄₄in6cm
Dwarf Corydoras	*Corydoras habrosus*	1¹⁄₄in/3cm
Dwarf or Pygmy Corydoras	*Corydoras hastatus*	³⁄₄in/2cm
Leopard Corydoras	*Corydoras julii*	2¹⁄₄in/6cm
Bandit or Masked Corydoras	*Corydoras metae*	2¹⁄₄in/6cm

RUMMY-NOSED TETRA
Hemigrammus rhodostomus and others

Various similar-looking species are referred to as Rummy-nosed Tetras. All have the characteristic red head and all are shoalers. Single specimens are often timid; groups are considerably more confident. Rummy-nosed Tetras associate well with Neon and Cardinal Tetras.

SPECIES DETAILS
Size: Around 1½ in (4cm)
Origin: Amazonia; the precise locality depends on the species

Ease of keeping: Moderately easy
Breeding: Egg-scatterer

AQUARIUM CARE
Water: Soft, acid water is preferred
Temperature: 72°–77°F (22°–25°C), but warmer conditions can be tolerated, particularly by Cardinal Tetras
Food: Most (small) commercial foods accepted

Rummy-nosed Tetras

NEON AND CARDINAL TETRAS
Paracheirodon innesi, P. axelrodi

Neon and Cardinal Tetras have, quite rightly, been among the most popular of egglaying species for many years. The red band on the Neon Tetra extends only halfway up the body, while in the Cardinal Tetra it extends all the way up to the head. Both Neon and Cardinal Tetras are shoalers and must not be kept either as single specimens or as pairs. Most Neon Tetras are now captive-bred.

Cardinal Tetra

SPECIES DETAILS
Size: Neon Tetra to about 1½ in (4cm). Cardinal Tetra to 2in (5cm), but usually considerably smaller
Origin: Neon Tetra: Upper Amazon. Cardinal Tetra: Upper Rio Negro
Ease of keeping: Easy
Breeding: These are egg scatterers and are unlikely to breed in community aquariums

AQUARIUM CARE
Water: Soft, acid water is preferred
Temperature: 72°–77°F (22°–25°C), but warmer conditions can be tolerated, particularly by Cardinal Tetras
Food: Most (small) commercial foods accepted

OTHER TETRAS
Numerous other small to medium-sized tetras are suitable for community aquariums, and the following is a small selection only. All species accept the general conditions outlined for Neon Tetras.

Common name	Scientific name	Size
Blind Cave Characin/Tetra	*Astyanax mexicanus*	3½in/9cm
Silver Tip or Copper Tetra	*Hasemania marginata*	1½in/4cm
Buenos Aires Tetra	*Hemigrammus caudovittatus*	2¾in/7cm
Glowlight Tetra	*Hemigrammus erythrozonus*	1¾in/4.5cm
Head-and-tail Light Tetra (Beacon Fish)	*Hemigrammus ocellifer*	1½in/4cm
Bleeding Heart Tetra	*Hyphessobrycon erythrostigma*	3¼in/8cm
Black Neon	*Hyphessobrycon herbert-axelrodi*	1½in/4cm
Flag Tetra	*Hyphessobrycon heterorhabdus*	2in/5cm
Lemon Tetra	*Hyphessobrycon pulchripinnis*	2in/5cm
Serpae Tetra	*Hyphessobrychon serpae*	1¾in/4.5cm
Emperor Tetra	*Nematobrycon palmeri*	2¼in/6cm
Congo Tetra	*Phenacogrammus interruptus*	3¼in/8cm
Penguin Fish	*Thayeria obliqua*	2¾in/7cm

Family: **Cichlidae**

ANGELFISH
Pterophyllum scalare

This popular species is available in numerous color forms and several fin configurations. Although they are generally peaceful, Angelfish are predators, so large specimens and small fish are not good tankmates.

SPECIES DETAILS
Size: Up to around 4³/₄ in (12cm), but often smaller.

Much larger specimens are encountered in the wild
Origin: Amazon basin
Ease of keeping: Moderately easy
Breeding: Eggs are laid on a vertical surface and guarded by the parents, which become highly territorial

AQUARIUM CARE
Water: Soft, slightly acid water is preferred, but a wide range tolerated
Temperature: 73°–81°F (23°–27°C)
Food: Most commercial foods accepted

Female Kribensis with young

KRIBENSIS
Pelvicachromis pulcher

This is a somewhat exceptional species because the females, although smaller and shorter finned, are every bit as colorful, or even more so, than males. Several species are available, but *pulcher* is the most popular.

SPECIES DETAILS
Size: Males: around 4in (10cm); females: around 2³/₄ in (7cm)
Origin: South Nigeria
Ease of keeping: Easy
Breeding: This is a cave spawner. The sex of the offspring may be affected by the pH (acidity/alkalinity) of the water, higher values seeming to favor females

AQUARIUM CARE
Water: A wide range of conditions tolerated, but see above for the affect of the pH (acidity/alkalinity) of the water on breeding
Temperature: 75°–82°F (24°–28°C)
Food: Will eat most commercial foods

Blue Angelfish

Family: **Cobitidae**

KUHLI LOACH
Acanthophthalmus kuhlii

A small, eel-like, attractively marked fish, which looks its best when kept in groups. Several other species, most notably Myer's Loach (*A. myersi*), are also available. There is great confusion, however, about the precise identity of some species.

Kuhli Loach

SPECIES DETAILS
Size: 4in (10cm)
Origin: Southeast Asia
Ease of keeping: Moderately easy
Breeding: Difficult and rather unlikely to occur in community aquariums

AQUARIUM CARE
Water: Most conditions, as long as they are not poor
Temperature: 75°–86°F (24°–30°C)
Food: Most foods are accepted, some of which should be of fast-sinking type and provided late in the evening

Tiger Barb

Family: **Cyprinidae**

TIGER BARB
Barbus tetrazona

This active and stunningly marked barb, which is also sometimes known as the Sumatra Barb, has now been developed into several color forms, including Moss (Green), Albino and Champagne. Tiger Barbs are renowned fin nippers when kept singly or in pairs. However, when kept in a shoal, as they should be, they become so involved in display among each other that they seem to forget their bad habits.

Dwarf Barbs

Champagne Tiger Barb

SPECIES DETAILS
Size: Around 6cm (2¼in)
Origin: Kalimantan (Borneo) and Indonesia (Sumatra)
Ease of keeping: Easy
Breeding: Like most Cyprinids this species is an egg scatterer

AQUARIUM CARE
Water: pH and hardness are not critical, except for successful fertilization of eggs, when soft acid conditions are required
Temperature: 68°–82°F (20°–28°C)
Food: Most aquarium foods are accepted

OTHER BARBS

Barbs vary considerably in size, and some are quite unsuitable for community aquariums. The following are all modestly sized and are well disposed for such systems, especially if kept in small shoals.

Common name	Scientific name	Size
African Two-spot Barb	*Barbus bimaculatus*	2¼in/6cm
Rosy Barb	*Barbus conchonius*	4in/10cm
Dwarf Barb	*Barbus gelius*	1½in/4cm
Ruby/Black Ruby/Purple-headed Barb	*Barbus nigrofasciatus*	2¼in/6cm
Odessa Barb	*Barbus "odessa"* *	2¼in/6cm
Checker/Island Barb	*Barbus oligolepis*	2in/5cm
Gold/Schubert's Barb	*Barbus "schuberti"**	2¾in/7cm
Cherry Barb	*Barbus titteya*	2in/5cm

* The origins of these two "species" is unclear. They are not found in the wild and are likely not to be true species at all.

ZEBRA DANIO
Brachydanio rerio

This beautiful, almost hyper-active shoaler prefers the upper reaches of the water column. Several varieties, including a long-finned and a golden type, are also available. The Leopard Danio (*B.frankei*) is now believed to be a single-gene mutant of the Zebra Danio.

SPECIES DETAILS
Size: About 2in (5cm)
Origin: Eastern India
Ease of keeping: Easy
Breeding: Egg-scatterer

AQUARIUM CARE
Water: With the exception of untreated tapwater, most conditions are tolerated
Temperature: 64°–77°F (18°–25°C)
Food: Most commercial foods, particularly floating types, are accepted
Special needs: Because the eggs are scattered and promptly eaten, a suspended mesh or a layer of largish pebbles or marbles on the bottom of the aquarium should be used to keep the parents from getting at them

Zebra Danio

FLYING FOX
Epalzeorhynchus kallopterus

This fast-swimming species spends much of its time darting between resting places. It feeds on algae which it scrapes off rocks and plants and, when resting, remains at the bottom of the tank supporting its body by resting on its dorsal fins.

SPECIES DETAILS
Size: 5¹/₂ in (14cm)
Origin: Kalimantan (Borneo) and Indonesia (particularly Java and Sumatra)
Ease of keeping: Moderately easy
Breeding: No documented reports of aquarium spawning are available

AQUARIUM CARE
Water: Reasonably tolerant of some deviation from soft, slightly acid conditions
Temperature: Should be maintained at 72°–81°F (22°–27°C)
Food: Most foods will be accepted, but should contain a vegetable component

Special needs: May become aggressive to members of own species, but leaves other occupants alone

HARLEQUIN
Rasbora heteromorpha

Of all the many Rasboras available today, the Harlequin, one of the oldest, is still among the most popular. Its peaceful, shoaling nature and character-istic dark, cone-shaped body patch have, no doubt, con-tributed significantly to its staying power.

Harlequin

SPECIES DETAILS
Size: About 1³/₄ in (4.5cm)
Origin: Malaysia and Thailand
Ease of keeping: Easy
Breeding: Unusually for a Cyprinid (most of which are egg scatterers), the Harlequin sticks its eggs on the under-surface of a leaf

AQUARIUM CARE
Water: It prefers soft, mature, slightly acid water
Temperature: 75°–81°F (24°–27°C)
Food: It will take most small commercial foods
Special needs: Should be kept in shoals

Flying Fox

Clown Rasbora

SOME OTHER RASBORAS

Common name	Scientific name	Size
Red-tailed Rasbora	*Rasbora borapetensis*	1³/₄in/4.5cm
Clown/Big-spot/Two-spot Rasbora	*Rasbora kalochroma*	4in/10cm
Dwarf/Pygmy/Spotted Rasbora	*Rasbora maculata*	1in/2.5cm
Glowlight/Red/Red-striped Rasbora	*Rasbora pauciperforata*	2¹/₄in/6cm
Scissortail/Three-line Rasbora	*Rasbora trilineata*	4³/₄in/12cm

Family: **Gyrinocheilidae**

CHINESE ALGAE EATER/SUCKING LOACH
Gyrinocheilus aymonieri

The most notable feature of this remarkable fish is that it has a special mouth and gill chamber arrangement that allows it to hang on to rocks in a fast-flowing current, breathe and feed all at the same time. Interestingly, it is not Chinese, as its name implies.

Golden Sucking Loach

SPECIES DETAILS
Size: Up to 9¹/₂in (24cm), but usually much smaller
Origin: Thailand
Ease of keeping: Easy
Breeding: Although it is commercially bred, there are no documented reports of aquarium spawnings

AQUARIUM CARE
Water: Not critical about water conditions, as long as oxygen level is reasonable
Temperature: 70°–86°F (21°–30°C)

Food: Most foods will be accepted, despite its reputation as a herbivore

Family: **Loricariidae**

PLECOSTOMUS CATFISH
Hypostomus, Liposarchus and Glyptoperichthys are still referred to in most books as *Pterygoplichthys*

The Plecostomus is a popular Suckermouth Catfish, usually sold when it is 3–4in (7.5–10cm) long. They are delightful fish, but they do grow rather large (see below). They are excellent algal grazers and are more active at night.

The species most often offered belong to the genera *Hypostomus, Glyptoperichthys* and *Liposarchus*. *Hypostomus* species have fewer dorsal fin rays.

SPECIES DETAILS
Size: 12–24in (30–60cm)
Origin: Tropical South America; some populations have become established in Florida
Ease of keeping: Easy
Breeding: Not known in aquariums. In the wild these species breed in burrows

AQUARIUM CARE
Water: A wide variety of water conditions, as long as the quality is not poor
Temperature: 68°–77°F (20°–25°C)
Food: Will accept most foods, but must include a vegetable component. Sinking food tablets, supplied in the evening, are strongly recommended

Golden Plecostomus

Banjo Catfish

OTHER CATFISH
There are countless species of catfish, many of which are suitable for first aquariums and many of which are not, the latter group usually, but not exclusively, including large predatory ones. Seek advice.

Common name	Scientific name	Size
Bristle-nose	*Ancistrus* spp.	5¹/₂in/14cm
Banjo Catfish	*Bunocephalus* spp.	3¹/₄in/8cm
Porthole Catfish	*Dianema longibarbis*	4³/₄in/12cm
Twig Catfish	*Farlowella* spp.	6in/15cm
Glass Catfish	*Kryptopterus bicirrhis*	4³/₄in/12cm
Otocinclus	*Otocinclus affinis*	2in/5cm

"COLDWATER" TROPICAL SPECIES

As we have already seen, the demarcation line between what constitutes tropical and "coldwater" tropical conditions is not sharp and clearly identifiable. As a result, many species can straddle the area between the two and are, in fact, perfectly capable of being treated as tropicals. Although low temperatures are accepted or tolerated by these species, any prolonged exposure to such conditions should be avoided.

The following list is a brief selection of those that you are likely to find widely available and which are deemed suitable for beginners setting up a community aquarium. Some have already been referred to in more detail in the freshwater tropical species section but are included here because of their tolerance of "coldwater" conditions.

Common name	Scientific name	Temperature range
LIVEBEARERS		
Family: **Poeciliidae**		
Mosquito Fish	*Gambusia affinis*; *G. holbrooki*	As low as 50°F / 10°C
Guppy	*Poecilia reticulata*	70°–77°F / 21°–25°C
Platy	*Xiphophorus maculatus*	70°–79°F / 20°–26°C
Sunset Platy	*Xiphophorus variatus*	61°–81°F / 16°–27°C
EGGLAYERS		
Family: **Belontiidae**		
Paradise Fish	*Macropodus opercularis*	61°–79°F / 16°–26°C (but as low as 50°F) / 10°C
Family: **Callichthyidae**		
Bronze Corydoras	*Corydoras aeneus*	64°–79°F / 18°–26°C
Family: **Characidae**		
Blind Cave Tetra	*Astyanax mexicanus*	64°–77°F / 18°–25°C
Family: **Cichlidae**		
Blue Acara	*Aequidens pulcher*	64°–77°F / 18–25°C
Family: **Cobitidae**		
Weatherfish or Weather Loach	*Misgurnus fossilis*	As low as 50°F / 10°C
Family: **Cyprinidae**		
Rosy Barb	*Barbus conchonius*	57°F / 14°C (winter only)
Tiger Barb	*Barbus tetrazona*	68°–82°F / 20°–28°C
Zebra Danio	*Brachydanio rerio*	64°–77°F / 18°–25°C
Fathead Minnow	*Pimephales promelas*	50°–77°F / 10°–25°C
White Cloud Mountain Minnow	*Tanichthys albonubes*	59°–77°F / 15°–25°C
Family: **Cyprinodontidae**		
American Flagfish	*Jordanella floridae*	66°–77°F / 19°–25°C
Family: **Loricariidae**		
Plecostomus Catfish	*Hypostomus, Glyptoperichthys, Liposarchus*	68°–77°F / 20°–25°C
Family: **Orzyiidae**		
Medaka	*Oryzias latipes*	58°–82°F / 15°–28°C

LIVEBEARERS

Family: **Poeciliidae**

MOSQUITO FISH
*Gambusia affinis and
G. holbrooki*

This small, guppy-like fish is the most widely distributed livebearer in the world, having been introduced into many tropical and subtropical countries to control malaria mosquitos. Two kinds of males occur, the more drab (and more common) wild type, and the mottled or totally black (melanistic) ones.

These species are ideal for beginners; they are tough and extremely easy to keep.

Mosquito Fish

SPECIES DETAILS
Size: Males around 1¼in (3cm); females around 2½in (6.5cm)
Origin: Originally, *G. affinis* was found in Texas and *G. holbrooki* in the eastern U.S. Both are now widely distributed elsewhere
Ease of keeping: Easy, but see note below
Breeding: Batches of around 50 fry every 5–8 weeks. Parents are highly cannibalistic

AQUARIUM CARE
Water: Tolerant of a wide range of water conditions
Temperature: From 50°–77°F (10° to over 20°C)

Food: All foods accepted
Special needs: Aggressive fin nippers, and care should be taken if they are kept with most other species, especially in communities

EGGLAYERS

Family: **Belontiidae**

PARADISE FISH
Macropodus opercularis

This species holds the honor of being the first so-called tropical fish introduced into Europe around 1869. It is a tough, hardy and very beautiful fish and, at least in these respects, it is an ideal beginner's fish. However, it is also aggressive, particularly at breeding time.

SPECIES DETAILS
Size: Around 4in (10cm), but usually smaller
Origin: Eastern China, Korea and Vietnam

Paradise Fish

Ease of keeping: Easy
Breeding: Males build bubble-nests, into which the eggs are deposited and which they guard with tremendous energy

AQUARIUM CARE
Water: Tolerant of wide-ranging water conditions
Temperature: 61°–79°F (16°–26°C). Even lower temperatures can be tolerated for a short time
Food: Most commercial foods accepted

Family: **Characidae**

BLIND CAVE TETRA
Astyanax fasciatus mexicanus

Also known as the Blind Cave Fish or Blind Cave Characin, this species can still be found in many books under its former name *Anoptichthys jordani*.

The most distinctive feature of the species is the absence of eyes: these are small at birth and become overlaid with tissue as the fish grow.

Blind Cave Tetras

Despite this apparent handicap, Blind Cave Tetras have excellent senses and can handle themselves perfectly well in an aquarium with other species.

SPECIES DETAILS
Size: Up to 3¹/₂in (9cm)
Origin: Mexico, Texas and Central America (to Panama)
Ease of keeping: Easy
Breeding: An egg scatterer

AQUARIUM CARE
Water: Not critical of water conditions
Temperature: 64°–77°F (18°–25°C)

Food: Will accept all commercial food

Family: Cichlidae

BLUE ACARA
Aequidens pulcher

Cichlid nomenclature is currently being revised and may result in this species reverting to its former name of *A. latifrons*
 This attractive medium-sized cichlid is tolerant of other species during most of its juvenile life. As specimens become older, however, they also become more aggressive.

SPECIES DETAILS
Size: Up to 7in (18cm), but usually quite a bit smaller
Origin: Colombia, Panama, Trinidad and Venezuela
Ease of keeping: Easy
Breeding: A typical substrate spawner, in which both parents guard the eggs and fry

Blue Acara

AQUARIUM CARE
Water: Tolerant of a wide range of water conditions
Temperature: 64°–77°F (18°–25°C)
Food: All commercial foods accepted

Family: Cobitidae

WEATHER LOACH
Misgurnus fossilis

This species, also known as the Weatherfish, is sometimes referred to as a living barometer, owing to its characteristic of becoming extra active at times of low barometric pressure. It can also use its intestine as an auxiliary respiratory organ, thus being able to tolerate poor water conditions.

SPECIES DETAILS
Size: Up to 6in (15cm) in aquariums; larger in the wild
Origin: Most of Europe, except Britain and Scandinavia
Ease of keeping: Easy
Breeding: There are no documented accounts of spawning in aquariums

AQUARIUM CARE
Water: Tolerant of a wide range of conditions
Temperature: As low as 50°F (10°C) and up to around 75°F (24°C).
Food: Will accept all commercial foods

Weather Loach

Family: **Cyprinidae**

ROSY BARB
Barbus conchonius

This active shoaler has now been developed into several color forms and hi-fin varieties. The males are more colorful than the females, particularly in breeding coloration.

Other species that, at first sight, look a little similar to the wild-type Rosy include the Ticto Barb, Cuming's Barb and Stoliczk's Barb.

Long-fin Rosy Barb

SPECIES DETAILS
Size: Around 4in (10cm)
Origin: Northern India, Assam, Bengal
Ease of keeping: Easy
Breeding: This is a typical egg-scattering species

AQUARIUM CARE
Water: Not critical of water conditions, as long as untreated tapwater is avoided
Temperature: Can tolerate a temperature range of 57°–59°F (14°–15°C) for a short winter period; 72°–77°F (22°–24°C) at other times
Food: All commercial foods are accepted

Fathead Minnow

FATHEAD MINNOW
Pimephales promelas

A relatively new introduction. It is a temperate-water fish but, because of its wide temperature tolerance range, it is fast gaining popularity among tropical aquarists. In its native U.S., it is largely regarded as a "bait" fish. In other countries, it is often sold as the Golden or Rosy/Red Minnow.

SPECIES DETAILS
Size: 4in (10cm)
Origin: Most of North America, but not on the Atlantic slopes south of the Delaware River; also found in northern Mexico
Ease of keeping: Moderately easy

Breeding: Eggs are laid on the underside of leaves and are guarded by the male

AQUARIUM CARE
Water: Not critical of water conditions.
Temperature: 50°–77°F (10°–25°C)
Food: All commercial foods are accepted

WHITE CLOUD MOUNTAIN MINNOW
Tanichthys albonubes

This delightful tiny species has been a strong favorite with aquarists for many years. It is hardy, peaceful and colorful and, although a little confusion still surrounds its scientific name, this has never stood in the way of its popularity. A long-finned, less hardy variety is also occasionally available.

SPECIES DETAILS
Size: About 1³/₄in (4.5cm)
Origin: Populations with whitish edges to the dorsal and anal fins come from

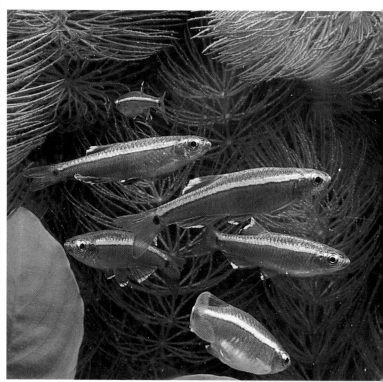

White Cloud Mountain Minnows

American Flagfish

Guangzhou (China); those with red edges are apparently aquarium-raised and originate from Hong Kong
Ease of keeping: Easy
Breeding: An egg-scattering species, which tends not to eat its own spawn

AQUARIUM CARE
Water: Water conditions not critical
Temperature: A highly adaptable fish that can comfortably handle a temperature range of 59°–77°F (15°–25°C)
Food: All small commercial foods are accepted

Family: **Cyprinodontidae**

AMERICAN FLAGFISH
Jordanella floridae

This killifish is unusual in that it can use two different reproductive strategies. Although it is a hardy species and there fore generally easy to keep, males are aggressive, particularly toward other males.

SPECIES DETAILS
Size: 2¹/₂in (6.5cm)
Origin: Florida
Ease of keeping: Moderately easy
Breeding: Eggs are laid, either among plants or, almost cichlid fashion, in a depression and are guarded by the male

AQUARIUM CARE
Water: Not critical of water conditions, although keeping tank filled with fresh water appears to be appreciated
Temperature: 66°–77°F (19°–25°C)
Food: All foods are accepted, but these should include a vegetable component

Family: **Oryziidae**

MEDAKA
Oryzias latipes

Other names for this active fish are Japanese Medaka, Golden Medaka, Rice Fish or Geisha Girl. Like the Mosquito Fish (*Gambusia affinis* and *G. holbrooki*), Medakas consume large quantities of mosquito larvae and pupae in the wild, thus acting as an effective biological means of controlling the spread of malaria.

SPECIES DETAILS
Size: Around 1¹/₂in (4cm)
Origin: Japan
Ease of keeping: Moderately easy
Breeding: Females will carry their fertilized eggs attached to their vent for a while after mating, subsequently depositing them among vegetation

AQUARIUM CARE
Water: Prefers neutral water (around pH7), but accepts some fluctuations
Temperature: 59°–82°F (15°–28°C)
Food: Most commercial foods are accepted

Golden Medaka

BRACKISH WATER SPECIES

Just as there is a gradual transition between coldwater and tropical temperatures, so there is an equivalent one between freshwater and marine environments, this "in-between" zone being referred to as consisting of brackish water conditions. Again, just as there are species of organisms that can tolerate temperatures between the coldwater and tropical regions of the spectrum, so there are many that either live in, or can tolerate, brackish water.

   The following table is a small selection of fish species that accept such conditions. Some have already been discussed in the sections covering tropical and "coldwater" tropical fish. Therefore, full individual entries for the additional species that are suitable, with some planning, for beginners, are included on the following pages. They are not all suitable for "average" community aquariums. The more difficult species are referred to in a later section.

	Common name	Scientific name
LIVEBEARERS		
Family: **Anablepidae**	Four-eyed Fish	*Anableps* spp.
Family: **Goodeidae**	Butterfly Goodeid *	*Ameca splendens*
Family: **Hemirhamphidae**	Halfbeaks	*Dermogenys* spp.
Family: **Poeciliidae**	Pike-top Livebearer*	*Belonesox belizanus*
	Mosquito Fish*	*Gambusia affinis, G. holbrooki*
	Sailfin Molly	*Poecilia latipinna, P. velifera*
	Guppy	*Poecilia reticulata*
	Sphenops Molly	*Poecilia sphenops*
EGGLAYERS		
Family: **Atherinidae**	Celebes Rainbow	*Telmatherina ladigesi*
Family: **Centropomidae**	Glassfish	*Chanda* spp.
Family: **Cichlidae**	Orange Chromide	*Etroplus maculatus*
	Green Chromide*	*Etroplus suratensis*
	Mozambique Mouthbrooder*	*Oreochromis mossambicus*
	Kribensis	*Pelvicachromis pulcher*
Family: **Cyprinodontidae**	American Flagfish	*Jordanella floridae*
Family: **Eleotridae***	Sleeper Gobies	*Dormitator* spp.
Family: **Gobiidae**	Bumblebee Gobies	*Brachygobius* spp.
	Mudskippers	*Periophthalmus* spp.
	Knight Goby	*Stigmatogobius sadanandio*
	Peacock Goby or Gudgeon	*Tateurndina* spp.
Family: **Lobotidae***	Tiger Fish	*Datnioides* spp.
Family: **Loricariidae**	Plecostomus (only a few species at the lowest end of the brackish range)	*Hypostomus, Glyptoperichthys, Liposarchus*
Family: **Melanotaeniidae**	Red New Guinea Rainbowfish	*Glossolepis incisus*
	Australian Rainbows (numerous species)	*Melanotaenia* spp.
Family: **Monodactylidae** **	Mono or Malayan Angel	*Monodactylus argenteus*
	Striped Finger Fish	*Monodactylus sebae*
Family: **Scatophagidae** **	Scat or Argus Fish	*Scatophagus argus*
Family: **Tetraodontidae***	Puffers	*Tetraodon* spp.
Family: **Toxotidae**	Archer Fish	*Toxotes* spp.

   * These species cannot be regarded as community fish because of their size, aggression or predatory instincts.
   ** These species prefer conditions nearer the marine, rather than the freshwater, end of the spectrum.
   Notes: Pure water, which is never encountered in nature, has a specific gravity of 1.000. For seawater, the SG varies, depending on the locality, around 1.020. While it is not possible to put an exact value on precisely what is meant by brackish water, SGs from around 1.005 to 1.015 can be regarded as brackish. An "average" value of 1.008 would be found acceptable by most of the listed species. If you are attempting to adapt a potentially brackish fish from freshwater to brackish water, do this gradually by slowly increasing the concentration of salt over a period of a week or two.

LIVEBEARERS

Family: **Goodeidae**

BUTTERFLY GOODEID OR AMECA
Ameca splendens

This fascinating species was responsible, almost on its own, for bringing this unique family of fish to the notice of European aquarists during the early 1970s. Although it has never been universally available, it is nevertheless sufficiently widespread, well known and hardy, to be well worth considering.

Butterfly Goodeid/Ameca

SPECIES DETAILS
Origin: Jalisco, Mexico
Size: Males around 3$^{1}/_{4}$in (8cm); females to 4$^{1}/_{4}$in (12cm) but almost invariably smaller
Ease of keeping: Moderate
Breeding: Females ovulate and nourish their embryos during their development. As a result, the 40 or so fry are large, and very well formed at birth

AQUARIUM CARE
Water: Prefers alkaline, medium-hard freshwater. If it is being considered for a brackish aquarium, the lower end of the spectrum will suit it best
Temperature: 70°-84°F (20°-29°C)
Food: All commercial foods will be accepted, but must include a vegetable component

Malaysian Halfbeak

Family: **Hemirhamphidae**

WRESTLING OR MALAYSIAN HALFBEAK
Dermogenys pusillus

These are elongated surface-swimming fish with fins set well back on the streamlined body. The "Wrestling" part of the name refers to the aggression that males exhibit toward each other, while the "Halfbeak" part refers to its unequal jaws, the lower one being considerably longer than the top.

SPECIES DETAILS
Size: Males around 2$^{1}/_{4}$in (6cm); females around 3$^{1}/_{4}$in (8cm)
Origin: Java, Indonesia, Kalimantan, Malaysia, Singapore, Sumatra, Thailand
Ease of keeping: Moderate to difficult
Breeding: Approximately 40 very large fry ($^{1}/_{3}$in/1cm) are produced every 4–8 weeks

AQUARIUM CARE
Water: Fresh or brackish conditions accepted. For brackish water, add about 1 teaspoon salt per 1.2 gallons (4.5 liters) freshwater
Temperature: 68°–86°F (20°–30°C)
Food: Floating foods accepted, but sinking foods will be largely ignored

EGGLAYERS

Family: **Atherinidae**

CELEBES RAINBOW
Telmatherina ladigesi

This delicate-looking species is at its best when kept in a shoal in a heavily planted aquarium provided with open swimming space. It is a peaceful fish, which should not be kept with boisterous fin nippers, such as barbs.

Size: 3in (7.5cm)
Origin: Sulawesi (formerly Celebes), Kalimantan
Ease of keeping: Moderately easy
Breeding: Eggs are scattered among fine-leaved vegetation and can take up to one week to hatch

AQUARIUM CARE
Water: Hardish water is preferred, with a little salt added (about 1 teaspoonful per 2.4 gallons/9 liters)
Temperature: 68°–79°F (20°–26°C)
Food: Will accept most foods

Celebes Rainbow

Family: **Centropomidae**

INDIAN GLASSFISH
Chanda ranga

In its proper setting this is a delicately beautiful fish. Other species of *Chanda* are available, and all require the same basic conditions. So-called Painted or Disco Glassfish and other species became available in large numbers during the 1980s. These fish, which,

Indian Glassfish

rather than being painted, are injected with a luminous dye that fades over a period of months, are still to be found, but growing resistance from aquarists and the aquatic industry is leading to a gradual decline in popularity, and they could become virtually unknown before long.

SPECIES DETAILS
Size: 2¼in (6cm)
Origin: Myanmar (Burma), India, Thailand
Ease of keeping: Moderately easy
Breeding: Difficult to achieve in aquariums. Eggs are scattered among vegetation and hatch in about 24 hours

AQUARIUM CARE
Water: Hard alkaline water is preferred, with up to 3 teaspoonsful of salt added to every 1.2 gallons (4.5 liters) of water
Temperature: 64°–77°F (18°–25°C)

Food: Some commercial foods are accepted, particularly deep-frozen ones, but live foods are preferred

Family: **Cichlidae**

ORANGE CHROMIDE
Etroplus maculatus

This is now available in three color forms: the wild type, a golden type and a rarely seen "blue" type. It is a peaceful species that will happily tolerate freshwater, but it prefers brackish conditions. The much larger Green or Speckled Chromide (*E. suratensis*) is much more difficult and, because of its potential size, 12in (30cm), cannot be regarded as a beginner's fish.

SPECIES DETAILS
Size: Up to 4in (10cm); usually smaller
Origin: India and Sri Lanka
Ease of keeping: Moderately easy
Breeding: Eggs are laid on a flat surface, and both they and the fry are guarded by both parents

AQUARIUM CARE
Water: Freshwater or (preferably) water containing 1–2 teaspoons salt per 1.2 gallons (4.5 liters)
Temperature: 70°–79°F (21°–26°C)
Food: All commercial foods are accepted, but there should also be a regular vegetable component

MOZAMBIQUE MOUTHBROODER
Oreochromis mossambicus

This must be one of the most adaptable, if not the most adaptable, of all cichlids. It can withstand anything from total freshwater to total marine conditions and is a prolific breeder. It is an important foodfish and is available either in the wild type form or as a golden/red/mottled one. Its hardiness makes it a fish that beginners should find easy to keep, although filtration must be good. However, it is too aggressive for most community aquariums.

Mozambique Mouthbrooder

SPECIES DETAILS
Size: Males to 15in (38cm); females smaller; both sexes grow considerably smaller in aquariums
Origin: East Africa
Ease of keeping: Easy
Breeding: Males will dig pits, to which they attract females. Up to 300 eggs may be laid, and these are incubated by the female in her mouth.

AQUARIUM CARE
Water: Anything from freshwater to marine conditions accepted
Temperature: 68°–75°F (20°–24°C)
Food: All foods will be accepted
Special needs: Good filtration

Orange Chromide

Spotted Sleeper Goby

Family: **Eleotridae**

SPOTTED SLEEPER GOBY
Dormitator maculatus

There are several species of Sleeper Goby available besides this one and all require the same basic treatment. Unlike other brackish species, *D. maculatus* does not adapt to freshwater. But it is hardy, predatory and generally easy to keep. A sandy bottom and caves are recommended for this territorial species.

SPECIES DETAILS
Size: 10in (25cm), but usually considerably smaller
Origin: Atlantic coast of tropical South America
Ease of keeping: Moderate
Breeding: Eggs are laid on a cleaned surface and protected. They hatch in about a day

AQUARIUM CARE
Water: Brackish or even totally saline conditions
Temperature: 72°–77°F (22°–25°C)
Food: Meat-based foods are preferred

Family: **Gobiidae**

BUMBLEBEE GOBY
Brachygobius xanthozona

Several species of *Brachygobius* are available, but it is often difficult to distinguish between them. All require the same conditions. This is a sedate, often timid fish which, despite its small size, is very attractive.

SPECIES DETAILS
Size: 1³/₄in (4.5cm)
Origin: Southeast Asia
Ease of keeping: Moderately easy
Breeding: Eggs are laid in caves and are guarded by the male

AQUARIUM CARE
Water: Brackish conditions consisting of 1–2 teaspoons of salt per 1.2–2.4 gallons (4.5–9 liters) of water
Temperature: 77°–86°F (25°–30°C)

Bumblebee Goby

Food: All kinds of small meat-based foods, especially live foods, are accepted
Special needs: Adequate cover in the form of rock caves

KNIGHT GOBY
Stigmatogobius sadanundio

This attractively spotted goby, although territorial (as most species of goby are), is quite a peaceful fish, which can be kept with other species, except very small individuals or any species that will compete with it for space.

SPECIES DETAILS
Size: Around 3¹/₂in (8.5cm)
Origin: Southeast Asia
Ease of keeping: Moderate
Breeding: Eggs are laid in caves and protected by both parents

AQUARIUM CARE
Water: While it will tolerate freshwater, this must never be soft and acid. Add 1–2 teaspoons of salt to every 1.2–2.4 gallons (4.5–9 liters) of water
Temperature: 68°–79°F (20°–26°C). Higher daytime and lower nighttime temperatures are recommended
Food: All types of live food – and many meat-based foods – are accepted

Knight Goby

Family: **Melanotaeniidae**

RED NEW GUINEA RAINBOWFISH
Glossolepis incisus

This is a truly impressive species in which males develop a pronounced hump behind their somewhat pointed head. They also exhibit a deep reddish coloration. Neither of these features is apparent in the females which are smaller.

SPECIES DETAILS
Size: Males up to 6in (15cm); females considerably smaller
Origin: Northern New Guinea
Ease of keeping: Moderately easy
Breeding: Eggs are scattered among vegetation, often of fine-leaved bottom types like Java Moss (*Vesicularia dubyana*) and take up to a week or so to hatch

AQUARIUM CARE
Water: Hardish water with a little salt added, about 1 teaspoonful per 2.4 gallons (9 liters)
Temperature: 22°–26°C (72°–79°F)
Food: All commercial foods are accepted

New Guinea Rainbowfish

AUSTRALIAN RAINBOWFISH
Melanotaenia maccullochi

There are numerous species and varieties of *Melanotaenia* Rainbows. *M. maccullochi* is included here merely as a typical example. Although the guidelines below apply to many of the other species and varieties available, it is always wise to check before you buy. *M. maccullochi* is also known as the Black-lined Dwarf or McCulloch's Rainbowfish.

SPECIES DETAILS
Size: About 2³/₄in (7cm); often smaller
Origin: Northern Australia
Ease of keeping: Moderately easy
Breeding: Eggs are scattered among fine-leaved vegetation and take 7–10 days to hatch at 77°F (25°C)

AQUARIUM CARE
Water: Not critical, but hardish water with 1 teaspoon of salt added to every 1.2–2.4 gallons (4.5–9 liters) preferred
Temperature: 68°–77°C (20°–25°C)
Food: Most commercial foods

Australian Rainbowfish

Family: **Monodactylidae**

MONO OR MALAYAN ANGEL
Monodactylus argenteus

The elegant, peaceful and active Mono is usually available as small individuals suitable for freshwater aquariums. As they grow, however, their need for salt in the water increases, and adults require true marine conditions for long-term health. Monos should be kept in shoals, whether as juveniles or adults.

Mono Angel

SPECIES DETAILS

Size: 4in (10cm) in aquariums; wild specimens grow much larger
Origin: Coastal waters from the Red Sea to Australia
Ease of keeping: Moderately easy
Breeding: No accounts of aquarium spawning are available

AQUARIUM CARE

Water: Increasing salinity must be provided as the fish mature, with fully marine conditions being provided by the time they approach their full aquarium size
Temperature: 75°–82°F (24°–28°C)
Food: All foods accepted, but some, at least, must be vegetative in nature

Striped Fingerfish

STRIPED FINGER FISH
Monodactylus sebae

This species is shorter (front to back) but taller, than its more common relative the Mono. It is also a little darker. Like the Mono, it is a shoaling fish.

SPECIES DETAILS

Origin: Tropical coastal waters of West Africa
Size: Around 8in (20cm) for wild specimens; considerably smaller in aquariums
Breeding: Very rare in aquariums

AQUARIUM CARE

Water: Increasing salinity must be provided as the fish mature, with fully marine conditions being provided by the time they approach their full aquarium size
Temperature: 75°–82°F (24°–28°C)
Food: All foods accepted, but some, at least, must be vegetative in nature

Scat/Argus

Family: **Scatophagidae**

SCAT OR ARGUS FISH
Scatophagus argus

There are several types of Scat available. Of these, only an East African Scat (*S. tetracanthus*), which can spawn in freshwater, merits full species status; the others are more likely to be varieties of the Common Scat.

SPECIES DETAILS

Size: Up to 12in (30cm); usually much smaller in aquariums
Origin: Coastal waters in the Indian and Pacific oceans
Ease of keeping: Moderately easy
Breeding: No documented reports of aquarium spawning are available

AQUARIUM CARE

Water: As long as elevated nitrite levels are avoided, this species is tolerant of a wide range of salinities
Temperature: 68°–82°F (20°–28°C)
Food: All foods are accepted

Family: **Tetraodontidae**

GREEN PUFFER
Tetraodon fluviatilis

Several species of *Tetraodon* are commonly available. Some, like the Green Puffer, will be happy in brackish water; others will not. Check in advance. As long as suitable water and diet requirements are met, Puffers are not difficult to keep. They are aggressive fin nippers, however, so they are far from ideal community aquarium inhabitants, although juvenile fish are more tolerant.

SPECIES DETAILS

Size: About 7in (18cm) but usually smaller
Origin: Southeast Asia
Ease of keeping: Easy
Breeding: Eggs are laid on the substrate and are protected by the male. Spawning in aquariums is rare

AQUARIUM CARE

Water: Freshwater is tolerated, but brackish conditions are preferred
Temperature: 75°–82°F (24°–28°C)
Food: Live foods, particularly snails, meat-based and vegetable-based foods, such as specialty sinking tablets, are accepted
Special needs: A densely planted aquarium with some open spaces is recommended

Green Pufferfish

MARINE SPECIES

The salinity requirements of some of the species referred to in the previous section, particularly Scats and Monos, change as the fish mature. They are, therefore, adaptable creatures, which can tolerate fluctuations in the chemical composition of their environment. Reef fish, on the other hand, come from stable ecosystems, where salinity hardly ever changes (except in the temporary pools that form between tides). They have, consequently, evolved without a biological need to be able to adapt to environmental fluctuations. As a result, their requirements are much more precise than those for their brackish water and freshwater counterparts, and they therefore set a greater challenge for new aquarists. For this reason,

beginners are often advised to steer clear of marines until they have obtained some experience with their more tolerant freshwater cousins.

There is a great deal of sense in such advice. It is not essential to begin, however, with freshwater species, and it is, indeed, perfectly feasible to begin with marines. In order to do so successfully, though, preparations must be more thorough and species selection more cautious.

The following table includes some of the species that will provide you with the best chances of success. All the species chosen are reasonably hardy and will tolerate some fluctuations in water quality. However, under no circumstances must this be seen as an excuse for laxity or complacency. It should be regarded as an excellent opportunity to learn the rules without causing undue hardship.

Numerous other species are

not difficult to keep once the basics of aquarium management have been mastered. They are not included here because they may be over-aggressive (like many Triggers), or not tolerant of frequent or marked fluctuations (like many Tangs), or too big (like many Angels), or may require large open swimming spaces (like Snappers), or could present a danger to the careless aquarist (like the Scorpionfish).

Such species are not completely out of the question for the well-prepared beginner, but they do restrict the breadth of experience that can be obtained with an aquarium stocked with a wider variety of inhabitants. It is this variety that can provide the best grounding in the art and science of marine aquarium-keeping and it is why the following fish have been chosen in preference to other, sometimes equally hardy, candidates.

The following list features a selection of those marines that are most suitable for the beginner. All the species are reasonably hardy and tolerant of some fluctuations in water conditions. Keeping marine species is more challenging than keeping freshwater, but by no means impossible. More detailed entries, for at least one member of each of the families listed below, are given on the following pages.

COMMON NAME	SCIENTIFIC NAME	COMMENTS
Family: **Bleniidae**		
Midas Blenny	*Ecsenius midas*	Hardy and endearing species
Family: **Cirrhitidae**		
Long-nosed Hawkfish	*Oxycirrhites typus*	Peaceful and hardy
Scarlet Hawkfish	*Neocirrhites armatus*	Bottom-dwelling community fish
Family: **Gobiidae**		
Lemon Goby	*Gobiodon citrinus*	Peaceful bottom-dweller
Yellow Goby	*Gobiodon okinawae*	Peaceful except toward own species
Neon Goby	*Gobiosoma oceanops*	Peaceful and beautiful
Family: **Labridae**		
Dwarf Parrot Wrasse	*Cirrhilabrus rubriventralis*	Small, peaceful, community species
Banana Wrasse	*Halichoeres chrysus and Halichoeres trispilus*	Peaceful community species

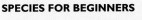

COMMON NAME	SCIENTIFIC NAME	COMMENTS
Cleaner Wrasse	*Labroides dimidiatus**	Delightful "cleaning" habits
Family: **Opistognathidae** Yellow-headed Jawfish	*Opistognathus aurifrons*	Peaceful burrow dweller
Family: **Pomacanthidae** Cherub Angel	*Centropyge argi*	Usually peaceful
Family: **Pomacentridae** Sergeant Major	*Abudefduf saxatilis*	Very active when young
Banded Clown or Anemonefish	*Amphiprion clarkii*	Variably-colored peaceful fish
Common Clown or Anemonefish	*Amphiprion ocellaris*	The one marine everybody knows
Green Chromis	*Chromis caerulea*	Hardy shoaler
Blue Damsel	*Chrysiptera cyanea*	Good, but territorial, shoaler
Yellow-tailed Damsel	*Chrysiptera xanthurus***	Hardy, but territorial, species
Humbug	*Dascyllus aruanus*	Tough, but territorial
Domino	*Dascyllus trimaculatus*	The characteristic spots fade with age
Family: **Serranidae** Wreckfish, Anthias or Lyre-tailed Coralfish	*Anthias squamipinnis*	Peaceful, colorful shoaler
Family: **Tetraodontidae** Valentine Puffer	*Canthigaster valentini*	Peaceful except toward its own species, but may nip long flowing fins

INVERTEBRATES		
Anemones	*Anthopsis, Condylactis, Heteractis, Stoichactis*	Many species are hardy and form excellent hosts for clowns
Fan/Tubeworms	*Sabellastarte* spp.	Good introductions to invertebrates
Shrimps	*Lysmata, Rhynchocinetes, Stenopus*	Colorful and relatively easy
Sea Apple	*Pseudocolochirus axiologus*	Easy if given adequate food
Starfish	*Fromia, Linckia, Pentaceraster, Protoreaster*	Not difficult if fluctuations are kept minimal and gradual

* The Cleaner Wrasse, while often regarded as a beginner's fish, must be well cared for in terms of food. If not, it will quickly deteriorate.
** There are many "blue" damsels available and all are basically territorial and hardy. Nomenclature is subject to revision, so expect the same fish to be available under more than one scientific name: *Abudefduf, Chromis, Chrysiptera, Pomacentrus*, etc.

Family: **Blenniidae**

MIDAS BLENNY
Ecsenius midas

Blennies are long, slender, active fish, which are generally hardy. Some species can be quite aggressive once they establish a territory in a preferred cave or burrow. The Midas is one of the more peaceful and is a good choice for a mixed species aquarium.

Midas Blenny

SPECIES DETAILS
Size: To (4in) 10cm
Origin: Indian Ocean and Red Sea
Ease of keeping: Easy
Breeding: Eggs laid and guarded in caves

AQUARIUM CARE
Water: Specific gravity between 1.021– 1.024
Temperature: 75°–79°F (24°–26°C)
Food: The Midas will accept all types of food
Special needs: Numerous rock shelters should be provided for all blennies

Family: **Cirrhitidae**

LONG-NOSED HAWKFISH
Oxycirrhites typus

Hawkfish are poor swimmers. They spend much of their time "perched" on a convenient lookout, from which they dart out to seize small swimming prey. Anything that is too large

Long-nosed Hawkfish

to swallow is generally ignored. Several species are available, including the spectacular Scarlet Hawkfish (*Neocirrhites armatus*), and all are quite hardy and can be kept with most other species of fish and invertebrates that are too large for the Hawkfish to eat.

Size: Around 4in (10cm)
Origin: Indian Ocean
Ease of keeping: Moderate
Breeding: Very rare in aquariums

AQUARIUM CARE
Water: Specific gravity between 1.021–1.024
Temperature: 75°– 79°F (24°–26°C)
Food: The diet should consist largely of meat-based foods
Special needs: Provide suitable lookouts or perches in the form of strategically placed rockwork

Family: **Gobiidae**

NEON GOBY
Gobiosoma oceanops

This striking little fish is now commercially bred in large numbers. Although they are quite hardy, Neon Gobies do not live longer than 18–24 months, not through any fault on the part of the aquarist, but simply because the species has a short lifespan.

SPECIES DETAILS
Size: To about 2¼in (6cm) in the wild; usually considerably smaller in aquariums
Origin: Western Atlantic
Ease of keeping: Easy
Breeding: Quite common in aquariums. Eggs are laid in caves and hatch after 7– 10 days. The fry are not difficult to feed on rotifers, followed by newly hatched brine shrimp

AQUARIUM CARE
Water: Specific gravity between 1.021–1.024
Temperature: 75°– 79°F (24°–26°C)
Food: A wide range of small-sized aquarium foods accepted. Eminently compatible with invertebrates
Special needs: Because they are so small, Neon Gobies should not be kept with potential predators

Neon Goby

OTHER GOBY SPECIES

The range of gobies currently available is somewhat more extensive than it was in the early to mid-1980s. Of these, several species are suitable for beginners, the following being the most commonly encountered ones.

Common name	Scientific name	Size
Lemon Goby	*Gobiodon citrinus*	1¼in/3cm
Bicolor Neon Goby	*Gobiosoma evelynae*	2in/5cm
Blue-banded or Catalina Goby	*Lythypnus dalli*	2in/5cm
Orange-spotted Goby	*Valenciennea puellaris**	6in/15cm
Blue-cheeked Goby	*Valenciennea strigata**	7in/18cm

* These larger species may disturb some invertebrates that live on or in sandy substrata.

Cleaner Wrasse "cleaning" a Butterfly

Family: **Labridae**

CLEANER WRASSE
Labroides dimidiatus

Although often recommended as a beginner's fish, the Cleaner Wrasse has specialized feeding habits. In the wild, it sets up home at a "cleaning station," to which other fish come to be relieved of parasites. In the aquarium, Cleaners will attempt a similar lifestyle, but neither the number of hosts, nor their parasites, can provide an adequate diet. Unless there is appropriate alternative food available, Cleaner Wrasse can starve to death, even in heavily stocked aquariums.

Cleaner Wrasse must, therefore, be treated as "special cases" and steps taken to ensure that they receive an adequate food supply at all times. If you cannot do this, do not buy a Cleaner Wrasse – other species are far easier. If you can, though, you will be richly rewarded.

Blue-cheeked Goby

SPECIES DETAILS
Size: Up to 4in (10cm)
Origin: Indo-Pacific
Ease of keeping: Moderately difficult, for the reasons mentioned above
Breeding: Unlikely in most aquariums

AQUARIUM CARE
Water: Specific gravity between 1.021–1.024

Temperature: 75°–79°F (24°–26°C)
Food: Small, meat-based deep frozen foods or live foods
Special needs: An adequate, alternative, food supply must be provided, in addition to its normal diet of the parasites on other community inhabitants

Clown Wrasse

OTHER WRASSES

There are numerous species currently available. Many, perhaps most, are offered as distinctly marked juveniles. Of these, relatively few remain small enough to be regarded as suitable community fish for beginners. For instance:

- **Twin-spot Wrasse** (*Coris angulata*) grows into the massive 48in (120cm) Napoleon Wrasse
- **Harlequin Tuskfish** (*Lienardiella fasciata*) attains 24in (60cm) in the wild
- **Birdmouth Wrasse** (*Gomphosus caeruleus*) grows to 10in (25cm)
- **Spanish Hogfish** (*Bodianus rufus*) can reach 8in (20cm) in aquariums and 24in (60cm) in the wild

More modestly-sized species to consider include the following:

Common name	Scientific name	Size
Dwarf Parrot Wrasse	*Cirrhilabrus rubriventralis*	3in/7.5cm
African Clown Wrasse	*Coris formosa*	Wild: 12in/30cm; Aquarium: 8in/20cm
Clown Wrasse	*Coris gaimardi*	Wild: 12in/30cm; Aquarium: 6in/15cm
Banana Wrasse	*Halichoeres chrysus* and *H. trispilus*	4in/10cm
Dragon Wrasse	*Novaculichthys taeniorus*	Wild: 8in/20cm; Aquarium: 3in/7.5cm

Yellow-headed Jawfish

Family: **Opistognathidae**

YELLOW-HEADED JAWFISH
Opistognathus aurifrons

A burrow-dwelling species, which requires a fairly deep bed of fine sand or gravel. It spends most of its time either half-in and half-out of its burrow, or hovering just above it. If the area of open substratum is large enough, several specimens can be kept in the same aquarium.

An invertebrate-compatible species, which is peaceful toward other species.

SPECIES DETAILS
Size: 5in (12.5cm) in the wild; usually smaller in aquariums
Origin: Western tropical Atlantic
Ease of keeping: Moderately easy
Breeding: Jawfishes are relatively easy to spawn in aquariums. Males brood the eggs in their mouths

AQUARIUM CARE
Water: Specific gravity between 1.021–1.024
Temperature: 75°–79°F (24°–26°C)
Food: Meat-based foods are preferred

Cherub Angel

Family: **Pomacanthidae**

CHERUB ANGEL
Centropyge argi

Also known as the Pygmy or Purple Fireball Angel, this is a generally peaceful species, which has been known to spawn in aquariums. Although the sexes are virtually identical, if two fish show clear interest in each other, it is reasonably safe to say that they are a pair.

SPECIES DETAILS
Size: Around 3in (7.5cm)
Origin: Western tropical Atlantic

Ease of keeping: Moderately easy
Breeding: Pairs will often spawn, releasing eggs into the water. Survival of eggs and fry are unlikely in most aquariums

AQUARIUM CARE
Water: Specific gravity between 1.021–1.024
Temperature: 75°–79°F (24°–26°C)
Food: The diet should include both a meat-based component and vegetable matter

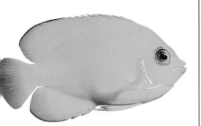

Lemonpeel Angel

Sergeant Major

Family: **Pomacentridae**

SERGEANT MAJOR
Abudefduf saxatilis

This attractively marked shoaling species is suitable for beginners during its juvenile stages. Adults tend to become aggressive and require considerable space, so large aquariums are preferable to small ones.

SPECIES DETAILS
Size: About 6in (15cm) in wild; usually smaller in aquariums

OTHER DWARF ANGELS
The Cherub and its closest relatives are usually referred to as Dwarf Angels, thus distinguishing them from larger types, like the *Holacanthus* and *Pomacanthus* species, which are not suitable for beginners. All Dwarf Angels attain lengths of 3–6in (7.5–15cm) in the wild, but they are often smaller than this in aquariums. They all require the same general aquarium care, with the emphasis being on good water quality. The following is a selection from the species available that would be well worth considering once the basic skills of water management have been mastered.

Common name	Scientific name	Comments
Fireball Angel	*Centropyge acanthops*	Peaceful grazer
Bicolor Angel	*Centropyge bicolor*	Generally peaceful; may be kept in groups
Coral Beauty	*Centropyge bispinosus*	Does best when adequate shelter provided
Eibl's Angel	*Centropyge eibli*	Subtly colored species
Lemonpeel Angel	*Centropyge flavissimus*	Predominantly herbivorous
Herald's Angel	*Centropyge heraldi*	Predominantly herbivorous
Flame Angel	*Centropyge loriculus*	Spectacular, rewarding species
Resplendent Angel	*Centropyge resplendens*	One of the easiest Angelfish
Pearl-scaled Angel	*Centropyge vroliki*	Adaptable and easy to feed

Flame Angel

Origin: Widely distributed in the Indo-Pacific region and tropical zones of the Atlantic
Ease of keeping: Moderately easy
Breeding: This is a substrate spawner, exhibiting parental care

AQUARIUM CARE
Water: No special requirements
Temperature: 75°–79°F (24°–26°C)
Food: Most commercial foods are accepted

COMMON CLOWN
Amphiprion ocellaris

The Common Clown is perhaps the best known marine aquarium fish in the world. Despite this, there is still confusion about its correct scientific name. A similar fish, referred to as the Percula Clown (*A. percula*) is also available, but *A. ocellaris* is the one most commonly encountered within the hobby.

Common Clown

Skunk Clown

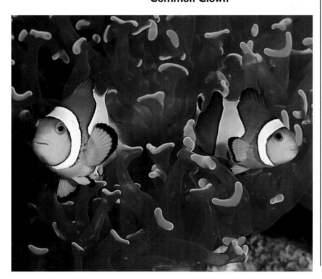

SPECIES DETAILS
Size: Around 3¹/₂in (8cm) in the wild; smaller in aquariums
Origin: Eastern Indian Ocean and western Pacific
Ease of keeping: Easy
Breeding: Eggs are laid around the base of the host anemone and are guarded by both parents

AQUARIUM CARE
Water: No special requirements
Temperature: Up to 78°F (26°C)
Food: Most commercial foods accepted
Special needs: Should be kept as a pair with a host anemone, such as *Heteractis* or *Stoichactis*

SOME OTHER CLOWNFISH / ANEMONEFISH

The following are the most widely available species of clownfish. All require the same basic care outlined for the Common Clownfish.

Common name	Scientific name	Size
Skunk Clown	*Amphiprion akallopisos*	Wild: 3¹/₂in/8.5cm; Aquarium: 2in/5cm
Two-banded or **Red Sea Clown**	*Amphiprion bicinctus*	Wild: 4in/10cm; Aquarium: 3in/7.5cm
Banded or **Clark's Clown**	*Amphiprion clarkii*	Wild: 4³/₄in/12cm; Aquarium: 2in/5cm
Fire, Red Saddleback or **Tomato Clown**	*Amphiprion ephippium*	Wild: 4³/₄in/12cm; Aquarium: 3in/7.5cm
Bridled, Fire or **Tomato Clown**	*Amphiprion frenatus*	Wild: 3in/7.5cm; smaller in aquariums
Black-footed Clown	*Amphiprion nigripes*	Wild: 4in/10cm; Aquarium: 2in/5cm
Pink Skunk or **Salmon Clown**	*Amphiprion perideraion*	Wild: 3¹/₂in/8cm; Aquarium: 1¹/₂in/4cm
Saddleback Clown	*Amphiprion polymnus*	Wild: 4³/₄in/12cm; Aquarium: 4in/10cm
Maroon Clown	*Premnas biaculeatus*	Wild: 6in/15cm; Aquarium: 4in/10cm

GREEN CHROMIS
Chromis caerulea

This beautiful shoaler has traditionally been referred to as *C. caerulea.* Most modern sources refer to it as *C. viridis,* however. Because "viridis" means green, this name appears to be the more appropriate. The Green Chromis is generally more peaceful than other damsels.

SPECIAL DETAILS

Size: Around 4in (10cm) in the wild; usually considerably smaller in aquariums
Origin: Widely distributed in the Indo-Pacific region; also in the Red Sea
Ease of keeping: Moderately easy
Breeding: Unlikely in aquariums

AQUARIUM CARE

Water: No special requirements
Temperature: Up to 78°F (26°C)
Food: Meat-based foods are preferred
Special needs: A gregarious, generally peaceful fish, which should be kept in a shoal

Blue Damsel

BLUE DAMSEL
Chrysiptera cyanea

This is one of several blue and blue-and-yellow damsels available. A hardy, territorial fish that becomes aggressive, particularly toward its own kind. Although found in large shoals in the wild, Blue Damsels are generally kept singly or in small groups in aquariums, the latter situation often leading to squabbles and hardship for the subordinate members of the shoal. Because they are hardy, damsels are often regarded as ideal fish to introduce into a new aquarium to speed up its maturation. This practice is to be discouraged, not just because it subjects the fish to raw, stressful conditions, but also because a resident damsel can make life difficult for fish subsequently introduced, even if they are considerably larger.

SPECIES DETAILS

Size: Around 2¼in (6cm)
Origin: Western Pacific and eastern Indian Ocean
Ease of keeping: Moderately easy
Breeding: A substrate spawner exhibiting parental care of the eggs. Spawning is, however, unlikely in most aquariums

AQUARIUM CARE

Water: No special requirements
Temperature: Up to 78°F (26°C)
Food: Most commercial foods are accepted
Special needs: Compatible with invertebrates, but not with its own species, unless kept in a shoal. See also main description

Green Chromis

DOMINO
Dascyllus trimaculatus

The immediately recognizable Domino is one of several distinctive *Dascyllus* species, including the Humbug (*D. aruanus*) and the False Humbug (*D. melanurus*). All require the same basic treatment as other Pomacentrids. The three white spots that give the Domino its dramatic appearance tend to fade with age.

Domino Damsel with anemone

SPECIES DETAILS
Size: About 5in (13cm) in the wild; smaller in aquariums
Origin: Indo-Pacific region and the Red Sea
Ease of keeping: Moderately easy
Breeding: A substrate spawner exhibiting parental care of the eggs. Spawning is, however, unlikely in most aquariums

AQUARIUM CARE
Water: No special requirements
Temperature: Up to 78°F (26°C)
Food: Most commercial foods are accepted
Special needs: Like other damsels, this is a territorial, invertebrate-compatible fish, which should be kept either singly or in shoals

Anthias

Family: **Serranidae**

ANTHIAS
Anthias squamipinnis

This elegant species is also known as the Wreckfish, Lyretail Coralfish, Golden Jewelfish or Marine Goldfish. While belonging to the same family as the giant groupers, *Anthias* is a delicate shoaler, which must not be kept as single specimens. *Anthias* is a good choice for a mixed fish/invertebrate aquarium.

Males are larger and more colorful than females.

SPECIES DETAILS
Size: Males 5in (12.5cm) in the wild; females smaller. Both sexes are usually smaller in aquariums
Origin: Indo-Pacific
Ease of keeping: Moderately easy
Breeding: No documented reports of aquarium spawning appear to be available

Valentine Puffer

AQUARIUM CARE
Water: No special requirements
Temperature: Up to 78°F (26°C)
Food: While preferring live food, this species will also take other foods, particularly if meat-based
Special needs: Must not be kept as a single specimen

Family: **Tetraodontidae**

VALENTINE PUFFER
Canthigaster valentini

The Valentine or Black-saddled Puffer is one of the so-called Sharpnosed Puffers, as distinct from the larger, more robust and more aggressive *Arothron* species. Nevertheless, other fish with long flowing fins may receive nips from this otherwise peaceful species.

SPECIES DETAILS
Size: Around 8in (20cm) in the wild; usually less than half this size in aquariums
Origin: Indo-Pacific
Ease of keeping: Easy
Breeding: No reports are available

AQUARIUM CARE
Water: No special requirements
Temperature: Up to 78°F (26°C)
Food: Meat-based foods are preferred
Special needs: Cannot be kept with invertebrates

INVERTEBRATES

ANEMONES
Anthopsis, Condylactis, Heteractis, Stoichactis

Anemones of the above genera are generally hardy and easy to keep, most species being particularly attractive to Clownfish, which will set up home among the stinging tentacles. Some *Heteractis* species may be found listed as *Radianthus* in older aquarium books.

SPECIES DETAILS
Size: From around 6in (15cm) for *Heteractis aurora*, to approximately 39in (100cm) for *Stoichactis gigas*
Origin: Tropical seas
Ease of keeping: Moderately easy

AQUARIUM CARE
Water: No special requirements but a constant flow required
Temperature: 75°–79°F (24°–26°C)
Food: Feed on small pieces of raw fish or shrimp once or twice a week

SELECTED ANEMONE SPECIES

Pink Malu Anemone
Anthopsis kaseirensis
Size: 4–12in (10–30cm)

Malu Anemone

Purple-based Anemone

Caribbean Anemone
Condylactis gigantea
Size: 6in (15cm)

Sand Anemone
Heteractis (Radianthus) aurora
Size: 6in (15cm)

Purple-based Anemone
H. (Radianthus) magnifica
Size: 28in (70cm)

Malu Anemone
H. (Radianthus) malu
Size: 4–16in (10–40cm)

Carpet or Blanket Anemone
Stoichactis gigas
Size: 39in (100cm)

FANWORMS OR TUBEWORMS
Sabellastarte spp.

There are several types of tube-, burrow- or rock-dwelling worms available. Some of these, like the rock- and coral-boring Serpulid species known as Christmas Tree Worms (*Spirobranchus giganteus*) have beautifully colored tentacles. However, a better and easier choice for beginners would be the larger and more subtly colored Sabellid species, particularly the Featherduster or Fanworm species, *Sabellastarte magnifica* and *S. sanctijosephi*.

SPECIES DETAILS
Size: The tube may extend 4in (10cm) or more above the substratum
Origin: Usually imported from the Far East
Ease of keeping: Moderately easy
Breeding: Fairly common in aquariums. Eggs and sperm are released into the water. Tentacles are often shed at this time and a new set regrown

AQUARIUM CARE
Water: Good quality water essential
Temperature: 75°–79°F (24°–26°C)
Food: Small, swimming or drifting types, like rotifers (*Branchionus*) or newly hatched brine shrimp (*Artemia*) or a fine-particle commercial mix

Fanworm

SHRIMPS
Lysmata, Rhynchocinetes, Stenopus

The variety of shrimps and their relatives, the lobsters and crabs, found today is quite extensive. Many, like most of the crabs and lobsters, can grow quite large or can be quite destructive. The various shrimps, therefore, represent far better choices for beginners, with some notable exceptions, such as the starfish-eating Harlequin or Orchid Shrimps (*Hymenocara elegans* and *H. picta*).

SPECIES DETAILS
Size: Body length $1\frac{1}{4}$–$3\frac{1}{2}$in (3–8cm), excluding antennae
Origin: Tropical seas
Ease of keeping: Moderately easy
Breeding: This is not uncommon in aquariums, but the larvae are generally difficult to raise

AQUARIUM CARE
Water: No special requirements
Food: All species accept a wide range of commercial foods
Special needs: Numerous shelters must be provided as retreats, particularly at molting time when shrimps are at their most vulnerable

Cleaner Shrimp

SELECTED SHRIMP SPECIES

Cleaner Shrimp
Lysmata ambioensis
"Cleans" fish of parasites in a similar way to the Cleaner Wrasse

Blood Shrimp
L. debelius
Spectacularly colored species

Dancing or Candy Shrimp
Rhynchocinetes uritai
Attractive hardy species with protruding eyes

Boxing Shrimp
Stenopus hispidus
The long main claws are brightly marked and waved in the water

SEA APPLES
Pseudocolochirus spp.

Despite the name, the Sea Apple is an animal. It belongs to the same group, the Echinoids, as sea urchins and starfish. Scientifically, the sub-group to which Sea Apples belong is known as Holothuroids. They are better known to aquarists as Sea Cucumbers.

SPECIES DETAILS
Size: 6–8in (15–20cm)
Origin: Indo-Pacific, but most imported specimens originate in Southeast Asia
Ease of keeping: Relatively easy, but see "warning" below
Breeding: Rare in aquariums

AQUARIUM CARE
Water: Current must be provided so that a flow of food can be carried to the tentacles
Food: Small planktonic live-foods or deep-frozen foods. Rotifers (*Branchionus*) and newly hatched brine shrimp (*Artemia*) are good food choices, supplemented by a suspension-type food. Feeding should be carried out at least once a day
WARNING: Holothuroids contain powerful toxins which they release when they are injured or die. Avoid housing them with strong stinging species

Blood Shrimp

Sea Apple

Blue Starfish

STARFISH
*Fromia, Linckia,
Pentaceraster, Protoreaster*

Starfish are available in a colorful and varied array of types, colors, sizes and degrees of difficulty. For new aquarists, the best types to consider are some of the more normal starfish. Crinoids (Feather Stars) and Ophuroids (Brittle Stars) are best avoided during the early stages of marine aquarium keeping.

SPECIES DETAILS
Size: Specimens are available from around 2in (5cm) to over 30cm (12in)
Origin: Tropical seas
Ease of keeping: Moderately easy
Breeding: Rare in aquariums

AQUARIUM CARE
Water: Good quality water
Temperature: 75°–79°F (24°–26°C)
Food: Small pieces of prawn, fish, squid or other types of "seafood." Food should be provided sparingly and should not be offered more regularly than once a day at most
Special needs: Smooth-armed species are less voracious than "knobbed" varieties, which are capable of consuming many species of sessile (fixed) invertebrates

Caution should be exercised, even with the smooth-armed types

SELECTED STARFISH SPECIES

Red Starfish
Fromia elegans
Bright uniform red species

Orange Starfish
Fromia monilis
Beautifully spotted orange/red species

Blue Starfish
Linckia laevigata
A spectacular old favorite

Common-knobbed Starfish
Pentaceraster mammillatus
Brownish-green with numerous knobs on the upper surface

Red-knobbed Starfish
Protoreaster lincki
Dramatically marked red and white species

Red-knobbed Starfish

SECOND-LEVEL SPECIES

The foregoing catalog of species recommended for beginners, although quite extensive, is far from exhaustive. This is to be expected, of course, since there are thousands of so-called aquarium species available throughout the world. Because a particular species does not figure in the catalog, it does not necessarily mean that it is unsuitable for beginners, so check with someone at the shop where you intend to buy your fish or with an experienced aquarist if you see a fish or an invertebrate that appeals to you but is not featured in the recommended list.

Having said this, however, there are other numerous species that, while not being impossible for beginners to keep, will nevertheless present a level of challenge that is probably best tackled after the basics of aquarium husbandry have been mastered. Many of these "second-level" species are beautiful and interesting and are hugely rewarding, but only if kept by someone who knows what their needs are and has the knowledge and experience to care for them.

FRESHWATER SPECIES

Perhaps the most "obvious" absentees from the species catalog are the widely available African rift lake cichlids, Discus, Oscars and the other Central and South American cichlids, along with many of the South American and African catfishes and a miscellaneous collection of Pencilfish, killifishes, knifefishes, large barbs, spiny eels and others.

African Rift Lake Cichlids

These can be found in an amazing range of colors,

Aulonocara "Eureka," an African rift lake cichlid

shapes and sizes. They are, in some ways, the freshwater equivalents of coral reef species, but they do have specific water requirements — that is, hard and alkaline. The provision and maintenance of such water conditions demand a degree of knowledge and expertise that, while not difficult to achieve, is nevertheless something that needs to be in place before any attempt is made to keep or breed these species. If you are fortunate enough to live in a hard, alkaline water area, you are already part of the way toward being able to keep African rift lake cichlids successfully.

A second factor adding challenge is that such cichlids are usually kept in heavily stocked aquariums with numerous rock shelters. Recommended stocking levels vary, but 50 percent over the average figures suggested for community tropicals is not uncommon. Ironically, such heavy stocking reduces the degree of aggression

toward individual fish that these species would exhibit under more normal conditions, but it increases the risk of water pollution.

Running such an aquarium successfully clearly demands more from the aquarist than a straightforward community system does.

Discus

These South American "aristocrats" of the aquarium also have very specific water requirements. They need soft, acid water, which, again, can be challenging to provide unless one lives in an area blessed with such conditions.

Pair of spawning Discus

Black-belt Cichlid

demanding requirements. Some may need hard, alkaline water (as do the various African *Synodontis*), or they may be predatory (an upward- or forward-pointing mouth armed with large barbels is usually a good clue here), or they may be secretive (as are cave-dwelling, twilight/ nocturnal grazers).

Together with cichlids, catfish constitute one of the largest groups of fish available to hobbyists. Not surprisingly, therefore, their needs vary enormously, so it is essential to seek detailed advice before purchasing any species that you cannot easily fit within the broad "community" category.

Soft water, by its nature, is low in dissolved salts, and a consequence of this is a distinct lack of buffering ("cushioning") capacity. As a result, any oversight – for example, overfeeding – can produce fluctuations in water quality that can spell disaster for the fish.

Oscars and other Cichlids

A variety of factors, ranging from size and territoriality (as with many of the Central and South American species such as Blackbelts, Jaguars, Oscars and Pike Cichlids), to habits (as with the Eartheaters, which constantly root around in the substratum), demand that most of these species be avoided by first-time aquarists.

African Catfish
Synodontis angelicus

Catfish

Many species, like most of the delightful *Corydoras*, can be easily kept and have already been mentioned. However, many other species have more

Predatory Catfish

Pencilfish and Killifish

Pencilfishes are delightful shoalers that are widely available. They are not difficult to keep as long as the chosen tankmates are not too boisterous (something that is quite common among community species, for instance, Tiger Barbs, Zebra Danios, etc.). They do, however, have a distinct preference for heavily planted aquariums containing soft, slightly acid water. In addition, their tiny mouths and generally retiring nature (particularly when faced with competitive feeders) make them more suitable for second, or species, rather than first aquariums.

The marked difference

between day and night color patterns in some species makes Pencilfishes very desirable, so do make a point of keeping them at some stage, but not at the very beginning.

One species of killifish, the

Shoal of Two-striped Pencilfish

Two male *Nothobrianchus* Killifish

American Flagfish (*Jordanella floridae*), was featured earlier in this book (see "Coldwater" Tropicals). There are, however, many other species of killifish that, while not as widely distributed in the hobby as some other types, are nevertheless seen often enough to offer temptation to the new aquarist.

Once their needs are known, killies are not particularly difficult. Many, though, have very specific requirements. Some are more temperate than others; some require peat-based aquariums; others spawn in mops. In many species, eggs need to be kept in damp peat for weeks or

months before they hatch. Males are often quite aggressive toward each other, yet the majority of species are timid and hide in community aquariums, often pining away. Numerous species are annual and live for only one season. Many are tiny fish, which need to be kept in small, specially set up single-species aquariums and so on.

Everyone should experience the delights of keeping killies at some time, but not during the earliest days of aquarium keeping.

Other Species
In addition to species that can be easily identified as small, desirable community fish, there is a whole host of others that can be surprising or may be either rare or unusual. For example, small Tinfoil Barbs (*Barbus schwanenfeldi*) grow at an alarming rate into large Tinfoil Barbs, which achieve 36in (90cm) in the wild, eating vast quantities of plants in the

Tinfoil Barb

process. Spiny Eels, Knifefishes and all manner of so-called oddball fish, including Swamp Eels, Reedfish, Silver Dollars, Pacus, Distichodus and Headstanders, all offer interest and challenges and are well worthy of consideration, but not at the beginning of one's aquarium career.

BRACKISH WATER SPECIES

As the number of aquatic shops offering brackish water

fish for sale increases, so does, quite naturally, the number of species. Some of the best and easiest have already been described earlier, but this leaves a number of regularly encountered, more challenging ones that are well worth considering as "second-level" choices.

Livebearers
Perhaps the ones that are offered more frequently than all others are the various unusual and amazing Four-eyed Fish (*Anableps* spp.). Some species can grow up to 12in (30cm) and this, along with their strictly surface swimming habits, dictates that they be kept in long aquariums with

Four-eyed Fish

ample space above the water for their extraordinary eyes to be fully appreciated. They are also jumpers, so their tanks must be kept covered.

Clearly, these are not ideal beginners" fish. Neither is the other livebearer occasionally offered: the highly predatory Pike-top Livebearer (*Belonesox belizanus*), whose cannibalistic tendencies, particularly in large, 8in (20cm) long females, can even extend toward their own mates.

Archer Fish
Like the Four-eyed Fish, Archerfish (*Toxotes* spp.) swim near the surface. Their eyes, while not protruding above the water, can nevertheless focus on small prey, like insects, perched on branches. They then proceed to shoot down their prey with strong

Archerfish

jets of water, which they can spit over considerable distances.

These fish make fascinating aquarium subjects, but they do require specially designed accommodation and a diet of live insects for their full range of behaviors to be admired.

Young Tiger Fish (*Datnioides microlepis*)

Tiger Fish
Two species of Tiger Fish are generally offered for sale: *Datnioides microlepis* and *D. quadrifasciatus*. Both are attractively marked in dark brown and white body stripes. Both grow quite large, the former attaining nearly 16in (40cm) in the wild; the latter, 12in (30cm), and both are highly predatory, having large eyes and mouths to prove it.

MARINE SPECIES

Among marine fish, the list of "second-level" species is long.

It is therefore quite impossible to cover it in any sort of detail here. What is possible, however, is to provide some general guidelines. If a species is excluded from those described in the species catalog given earlier, you should, at the very least, seek advice from your retailer and/or an experienced marinist before you decide to buy it.

MARINE FISH

Butterflies and Angelfish
Notable exclusions from the catalog are Butterflyfish (family, Chaetodontidae) and the larger Angelfish (family, Pomacanthidae) such as the *Euxiphipops*, *Pomacanthus*

Lemonpeel Butterfly

and *Holacanthus* species. This is not because they are all difficult or impossible (indeed, quite the opposite in many cases – although there are undoubtedly some difficult and "virtually impossible" species), but because of their relatively large size, their sometimes aggressive nature and demanding requirements when compared with genuine beginners" choices.

As in the case of killifish, every aquarist should keep Butterflyfish and Angelfish at some stage. They have tremendous qualities and beauty and, in the case of most Angelfish, dramatically different juvenile and adult phases. However, to avoid suffering by both the fish and yourself, you would be well advised not to rush in and stock up on these magnificent fish at the outset. Later, when you feel you are ready, ask about suitable choices.

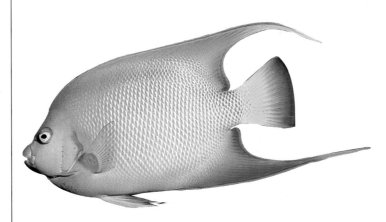

Queen Angel
(*Holacanthus ciliaris*)

Lionfish (*Pterois volitans*)

Lionfishes

Virtually anyone who keeps marine subjects wants a Lionfish, and with good reason. They are superb creatures with an aura about them that few other fish can match. Two genera of Lionfish are available: *Pterois* and *Dendrochirus*. All are beautiful, all are predatory and, very importantly, all carry venomous spines, which can cause excruciating pain to the unwary aquarist. Lionfish are generally not too difficult to keep, but they must be handled with extreme care. You can swim perfectly safely with them in the wild and you can keep them perfectly safely in aquariums, but at no stage can you afford to become complacent.

Blue Tang

Surgeons and Tangs

Many species are bold feeders, which adapt well to captivity, provided that the diet contains vegetable matter (many experienced hobbyists use lettuce for this). They can be quarrelsome, especially toward their own type, and, as the name suggests, carry scalpel-like spines on either side of their tail base. These can inflict injuries during territorial disputes or when used in defense, so, as with Lionfish, handle with extreme care!

In addition, Surgeons and Tangs need good water quality conditions; otherwise they may become susceptible to parasitic conditions such as white spot (*Cryptocaryon*).

Triggerfish

The unusual position of their eyes is a biological "must" to enable these fish to feed

Picasso Triggerfish

safely on long-spined urchins. These fish have a tough, often spectacular appearance.

Triggerfish are large – around 12in (30cm) is not uncommon – uncompromising, all-consuming fish, which can quite easily rearrange your tank decor overnight. By all means, keep one when you can, but prepare well for the experience.

Male Pacific Boxfish

Other Fish Species

There is a long list of species that, for one reason or another – from water quality demands to dietary habits – warrant a degree of expertise usually above that possessed by complete beginners. These include Box and Trunkfish, Mandarins, Dragonets, Groupers, Morays, Sweetlips, Basslets or Dottybacks, pygmy Basslets, many Wrasse,

Porcupine fish (*Diodon liturosus*)

Squirrelfish, Rabbitfish, most Puffers, Porcupinefish and others. Generally speaking, all of these can be kept in an aquarium, but some are more suitable than others, and a number of them fall within the "very difficult" category. Once again, it is important to seek appropriate advice once you feel you are ready to move on from your first aquarium to a more varied and demanding one.

MARINE INVERTEBRATES

Coral Relatives
The vast majority of "hard corals" are not recommended, even as "second-level" species. Indeed, some are exceedingly difficult to maintain for long

Green Polyps Coral

periods and present a challenge for all aquarists, irrespective of level of expertise.

Corals are scientifically classified, along with their relatives, as Cnidaria. Some of these related species represent good subjects for aquarists with some experience in keeping aquariums. Most notable among these are Mushroom Polyps (*Rhodactis* spp.), Green Polyps (*Zoanthus sociatus*), "soft corals" like the Pulse Corals (*Anthelia glauca* and *Xenia* spp.), Red Cauliflower (*Dendronephthya rubeola*),

Soft coral (*Dendronephthya* sp.)

Giant *Tridacna* Clam

Leather Coral (*Sarcophyton tracheliophorum*) and others. All require really good lighting to thrive.

Mollusks
Snails, scallops and clams are often offered for sale, and some can be maintained with varying degrees of difficulty. Flame Scallops (*Lima scabra*), for example, can be kept, once appropriately anchored, as long as a plentiful supply of fine-particle food is offered and no predators that might take a liking to its numerous tentacles are present.

Clams, such as the giant Tridacnas (*Tridacna* spp.), which are now commercially produced in large quantities, are filter feeders, and they can be kept if an appropriate diet is provided, along with top-

quality high-intensity lighting.

In general, snails and slugs are best approached with caution, because the specialized diets of many species could make life difficult or impossible for other invertebrates. For example, some Cowries (*Cypraea* spp.) show a distinct liking for corals. Similarly, many of the Dorid Sea Slugs, like *Chromodoris quadricolor*, will feed on a wide range of invertebrates. On the other hand, Sea Hares (*Aplysia* spp.) are herbivorous and do well once they settle down, while the Queen Conch (*Strombus*

Crinoids

gigas), now produced in large numbers on special farms, is not difficult to grow to around 10in (25cm).

Echinoderms

Brittle Star

With the exception of the Sea Apples and selected starfish described earlier, most other species are demanding. Crinoids or Feather Stars (*Himenometra* and others), sea urchins (*Echinometra, Diadema, Heterocentrotus* – the so-called Pencil Urchin – and many others). Brittle Stars (*Ophiomastrix*) and Basket Stars (*Astrophyton* spp.) are all "keepable," but only if their specific dietary and husbandry requirements are met.

Living rock

Sea Squirts (many species) and other invertebrates are often available, either as individual specimens, clusters or as part of living rock – that is, rock encrusted with and/or bored by invertebrates and algae.

Until fairly recently, all living rock was collected and harvested from the wild, and while there never appeared any risk of overexploitation, there was some controversy about its sale. Today, several commercial operators cultivate and harvest living rock on a sustainable basis, and sales of pieces collected in the wild are controlled by license in a number of countries.

One of the great attractions of good quality living rock is the diversity of different life forms it contains. Another is that it looks attractive, while yet another is its beneficial influence in helping to maintain healthy tank conditions. It can, however, present difficulties if some of the inhabitants die, either in transit or when rocks are introduced into the aquarium. For this reason, careful, efficient handling and maintenance are essential.

SPECIES FOR EXPERIENCED AQUARISTS

As with many of the other categories already discussed in this book, the dividing line between what constitutes a "second-level" species and one that should be reserved until the time one can be regarded as an experienced aquarist is a fuzzy one. Making the decision requires both judgment and common sense. By definition, there is an inevitable, and easily recognizable, gap between what constitutes a brand-new aquarist and an experienced one. Yet both will come across the same species in shops, and while the latter may be able to handle the husbandry that "advanced" species demand, it would be unreasonable and unfair to expect the new aquarist to be able to do so. Indeed, there are some species that even most experienced aquarists find challenging and several that, at the moment at least, are difficult or virtually impossible to keep for any length of time, irrespective of one's ability. The following deals with both types.

FRESHWATER SPECIES

Because freshwater systems are generally easier to establish and maintain than brackish or marine ones, water chemistry is not usually the main criterion by which fish are categorized as difficult or reserved exclusively for experienced aquarists only. Eventual size, and/or diet are, however, very significant.

If the specimen in question is already large when it is offered for sale, the evidence

Giant Gourami

speaks for itself. In many cases, however, large species are sold as juveniles, so unless you know what you are buying, you could easily and quickly end up with a sizable problem on your hands.

In some countries, retailers use special "large fish" labels to indicate the eventual size that a species exhibited will attain. If such labels are not displayed in the shop, ask for size guidance before you buy.

Among the large species encountered as juveniles are the Giant Gourami (*Osphronemus goramy*); Snakeheads (*Channa* spp.); Pacus (*Colossoma* spp.); Piranha (*Serrasalmus* spp.); Red-tailed Catfish (*Phractocephalus hemioliopterus*); Shovel-nosed Catfish (*Sorubim, Brachyplatystoma* spp. and others); Walking Catfish (*Clarias batrachus*); Arowana (*Osteoglossum* spp.); Dragon Fish (*Scleropages formosus*); Arapaima (*Arapaima gigas*); Electric Eels (*Electrophorus electricus*) and numerous others.

BRACKISH WATER SPECIES

Some brackish species, such as Target Fish (*Terapon jarbua*) and Soles (for example, *Achirus*), are only rarely seen, although Soles are gradually becoming a little more widely available and could, perhaps, be regarded as a "second-level" species. Occasionally, juveniles of species that, as adults, are marine are also encountered (in addition to Scats and Monos discussed earlier in the book). Mullets (*Mugil* spp.) and European Sea Bass (*Dicentrarchus labrax*) are among these. Such species should definitely not be considered by first-time aquarists.

By far the most common brackish water species offered for sale are the various delightful Mudskippers

Mudskipper (*Periophthalmus papilio*)

(*Periophthalmus* spp.). Coming from estuarine flats and mangrove swamps, these unusual gobies require an area of land – a "shore" – onto which they can climb and feed. In addition, the air in the aquarium must be kept humid and at a temperature similar to that of the water. Mudskippers are interesting fish, which, with due care, attention to detail and experience, can be kept successfully in an aquarium.

MARINE SPECIES

There are more "difficult" marine species, both of fish and invertebrates, than in all other categories put together. Undoubtedly, the fact that certain pollutants, such as ammonia, are highly toxic under marine conditions is a major contributing factor. However, since ammonia and other components can be controlled through appropriate husbandry, these cannot be considered to be the most significant limiting factors. Precise dietary or environmental requirements – lighting of a specific type and intensity, for example – combined with our current lack of knowledge about many species and their precise needs, or our inability to provide for these needs even if we know what they are, contribute toward making some marine species extremely difficult.

The question arises whether we should even attempt to keep such species in an aquarium. The answer is not a straightforward one, and there are advocates on both sides. Progress is, however, constantly being made, and even species that were once almost impossible to keep (such as sponge-feeding Butterflies) can now be maintained with relative ease because of the development of sponge-containing frozen foods (the sponge species used in these foods are very abundant, so there are no conservation implications).

Among the difficult species of fish most often encountered are seahorses (*Hippocampus* spp.). Everybody, it seems, wants to own a seahorse, but if you are a beginner, resist the temptation. Seahorses can be kept in aquariums, and they can even be bred, but they require very special care and a constant supply of small live foods like brine shrimp (*Artemia*) to survive.

Coral-feeding species of Butterfly, such as the Triangular Butterfly (*Chaetodon triangulum*), the Chevron Butterfly (*C. trifascialis*) and the Redfin Butterfly (*C. trifasciatus*), are just three of a selection of *Chaetodon* species that will be found challenging even by aquarists with many years' experience. Then there is the unusual Pine-cone Fish (*Monocentrus japonicus*), with its built-in light-emitting organ, the elegant and delicate

Seahorses (*Hippocampus* sp.)

Moorish Idol (*Zanclus canescens*), the headstanding Shrimpfish or Razorfish (*Aeoliscus strigatus*), the extremely venomous Stonefishes (*Synanceja* spp.), the slender Pipefishes (*Dunkerocampus* spp.), the larger or more difficult Morays (*Muraena* spp.) and so on.

Among invertebrates, the ones that stand out above all others as requiring the attentions of experienced aquarists are the hard or stony corals.

Numerous species are available, and none could be regarded as good choices for the new aquarist. All demand great attention to detail and some are difficult even for experienced hobbyists.

Other invertebrates that should be regarded with reservation include free-swimming mollusks like Squid (*Loligo* spp. and others); Octopi, particularly the beautiful, but potentially lethal, Blue Ring Octopus (*Hapalochlaena maculosa*); cuttlefish; Mantis or Pistol Shrimps; Cone Shells (which have a poison-laden dart); Fireworms (*Hermodice carunculata*), whose bristles can become embedded in the skin and cause painful rashes; starfish-eating Harlequin Shrimps (*Hymenocara* spp.) and a whole host of other species.

These may all be found from time to time, and all will be tempting. All must be resisted unless they can be adequately cared for.

Acropora coral on a reef in the Philippines

PLANTS

Plants perform some very useful functions in aquariums. Some are purely decorative, while others offer shelter for fry or retiring fish and invertebrates, or provide suitable spawning sites. Less visible, but just as important in many ways, are the buffering or cushioning effects aquatic plants have on water conditions. As already mentioned, they are able to absorb nitrates – the end product of the nitrification process carried out by beneficial "filter" bacteria – as well as generate oxygen and absorb carbon dioxide through photosynthesis during hours of illumination.

The following table lists some of the most common genuinely aquatic plants available for aquariums. In addition, there are "aquarium," as opposed to "aquatic" plants, which are terrestrial species that look attractive but have limited lifespans underwater.

FRESHWATER AND BRACKISH* SPECIES

* While these plants may be used in brackish water aquariums with varying degrees of success, they are not equipped to withstand high salinities. Therefore, the closer such aquariums get to marine conditions, the fewer the tolerant species and the shorter the lifespan. In freshwater, they live indefinitely if their other requirements are met.

FLOATING PLANTS

FAIRY MOSS
Azolla caroliniana

Coldwater/ tropical
Water: Medium hard
Lighting level: High

Fairy Moss

INDIAN FERN/WATER SPRITE
Ceratopteris thalictroides

Coldwater/ tropical
Water: Soft to medium hard
Lighting level: High
Also grows as a rooted plant

Indian Fern

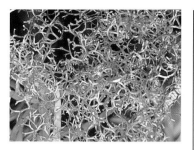

Riccia

RICCIA/CRYSTALWORT
Riccia fluitans

Coldwater/tropical
Water: Medium hard
Lighting level: High

Salvinia

SALVINIA
Salvinia spp.

Tropical
Water: Medium hard
Lighting level: High

ROOTED PLANTS

DWARF ANUBIAS
Anubias nana

Tropical
Water: Not critical
Lighting level: Low

Dwarf Anubias

Aponogeton

APONOGETONS
Various species of *Aponogeton*

Tropical
Water: Soft
Lighting level: Moderately low

Bacopa

BACOPA
Various species of *Bacopa*

Coldwater/tropical
Water: Not critical
Lighting level: Moderately high

CABOMBA
Various species of *Cabomba*

Coldwater/tropical
Water: Soft
Lighting level: High

Red Cabomba

HORNWORT*
Ceratophyllum demersum
and *C. submersum*

Coldwater/tropical
Water: Not critical
Lighting level: Not critical

Hornwort

Crypto

CRYPTOS
Various species of
Cryptocoryne

Tropical
Water: Soft
Lighting level: Low to
moderate

"Marble Queen" Amazon Sword

AMAZON SWORD PLANTS*
Various species of *Echinodorus*

Tropical
Water: Not critical
Lighting level: Moderately
high

Argentine Waterweed

ARGENTINE WATERWEED
Egeria densa

Coldwater/tropical
Water: Not critical
Lighting level: High

Hair Grass

HAIR GRASS
Eleocharis acicularis

Coldwater/tropical
Water: Not critical
Lighting level: Moderate to
high

CANADIAN PONDWEED*
Elodea canadensis

Coldwater/tropical
Water: Not critical
Lighting level: High

Water Wisteria

WATER WISTERIA
Hygrophila difformis

Tropical
Water: Soft
Lighting level: High

Indian Water Star "Rosanervig"

INDIAN WATER STAR*
Hygrophila polysperma

Coldwater/tropical
Water: Soft to medium hard
Lighting level: High

**Canadian
Pondweed**

Ludwigia

LUDWIGIA
Various species of *Ludwigia*

Coldwater/tropical
Water: Not critical
Lighting level: High

Java Fern

JAVA FERN*
Microsorum pteropus

Tropical
Water: Not critical
Lighting level: Low to moderate

WATER MILFOIL
Various species of *Myriophyllum*

Coldwater/tropical
Water: Slightly hard to hard
Lighting level: High

Tape Grass

TAPE GRASS/EEL GRASS/VALLIS
Vallisneria spiralis,
V. "Torta" and others

Coldwater/tropical
Water: Not critical
Lighting level: High

JAVA MOSS*
Vesicularia dubyana

Coldwater/tropical
Water: Not critical
Lighting level: Not critical

Java Moss

Two types of Water Milfoil

MARINE SPECIES

CAULERPA
(several species)
*Caulerpa mexicana,
C. prolifera, C. racemosa,
C. taxifolia,* and others
Lighting level: High

TURTLE WEED
Chlorodesmis fastigiata
Lighting level: High

Cactus Seaweed

Coralline Seaweed

VELVET SEAWEED
Codium gepii
Lighting level: High

CORALLINE SEAWEED
Corallina officinalis and others
Lighting level: High

CACTUS SEAWEED
Halimeda spp.
Lighting level: High

PAINT/SHAVING BRUSH SEAWEED
Pencillus capitatus
Lighting level: High

SARGASSUM
Sargassum spp.
Lighting level: High

SAILOR'S EYEBALLS
Valonia ventricosa
Lighting level: High

Note: In addition, other green (*Chlorophyceae*), red (*Rhodophyceae*) and brown (*Phaeophyta*) algae (seaweeds are macro-algae) are imported regularly, and all are worth trying, although in some cases success may prove elusive.

Acknowledgments

The publishers would like to thank the following for permission to reproduce the photographs and illustrations indicated below: Alternative Design Studio 9b, 11b, 12t, 13t, 20t, 26, 27, 40, 41t. Aqua Press - MP & C Piednoir © 9t, 13, 23, 31, 37, 38, 39, 43l, 44tl, cl, 45, 48l, 49tl, 50t, 51t, 52, 53c, 55tr, 56 l,t,b, 57t, 58cr, 60t, 61t,br, 66r, 67, 68b, 69r, 72l, 73r, 76, 77b, 80, 81t, 82t, 83, 85b, 86tl, cr, 88, 89l, 90l, 91tl, 92, 93. Dennis Barrett © 63b. Garth Blore © 34, 35. Dr Peter Burgess © 44bl, br. John Dawes © 12r, 16, 24b, 58cl, 60c, 65c, 73l, 82b, 85tr, 86bl. Harry Grier/Florida Tropical Fish Farms Association © 9t, 17r, 20, 49b,cr, 50tr, br, 51c, 55tl, 56tr, 62c, 63t, 65t, 66l. Linda Lewis © 44tl, 78b,l, 84c, 87c, 90c. Trevor MacDonald © 7, 8, 14b, 75r, 86tr, 94l,r. Bill Tomey ©10, 12l, 17l, 19, 21, 24t, 28, 30, 36, 43r, 44tr, cl, 48r, 49tr, 51b, 53t, 54, 55b, 57t, 58tl, br, 65b, 68l, 69l,c, 72r, 73b, 74, 75tl, cl, 77t, 78t, 79, 81b, 84tl, cl, r, 85tl, 87l, 89r, 91c, cr.

INDEX